THE GREATNESS OF SIVA

MAHIMNASTAVA

OF

PUSPADANTA

THE GREATNESS OF SIVA

MAHIMNASTAVA

OF

PUSPADANTA:

WITH THE COMMENTARY OF
JAGANNATHA CHAKRAVARTI

TRANSLATED WITH COMMENTARY

ARTHUR AVALON

GYAN

Published by

Gyan Publishing House
5, Ansari Road
Daryaganj, New Delhi-110002
Phone: 011-47034999, 9811692060
E-mail: books@gyanbooks.com

Distribution Network
gyanbooks.com
India, USA, Canada, UK, Australia

ISBN: 978-93-6920-415-1 (PB)

First Published, 1953

2nd Impression 2025

Printed at: Gyan Press, Delhi.

THE GREATNESS OF SIVA MAHIMNASTAVA OF PUSPADANTA
Author: ARTHUR AVALON

MAHIṀNASTAVA

THE GREATNESS OF S'IVA

MAHIṀNASTAVA

OF

PUṢPADANTA

WITH THE COMMENTARY OF

JAGANNĀTHA CHAKRAVARTĪ

TRANSLATED WITH COMMENTARY

BY

ARTHUR AVALON

(Third Edition, revised and enlarged)

TOGETHER WITH THE SANSKRIT COMMENTARY OF

SĀRĀRTHADĪPIKĀ

PUBLISHERS :

GANESH & Co., (MADRAS) LTD., MADRAS—17

1953

PRINCIPLES OF TANTRA

TRANSLATED BY

CONTENTS

Part I

Part II

INTRODUCTION

THE celebrated and ancient Hymn called Mahimnastava here translated is attributed to Puṣpadanta a Chief of the musical Spirits (Devayoni) called Gandharvas. Puṣpadanta means "flowery toothed" for his teeth were like the petals of the Jasmine flower. Puṣpadanta was, it is said, in the habit of taking flowers from the garden of King Vahu at Benares in order to worship S'iva with them. As he had the power of moving in the air he eluded the vigilance of the King's gardeners. These at length suspecting that it was some Being with these powers who stole the flowers laid the following trap. They left some flowers which had been offered to S'iva in different places in the garden with the hope that he, who thus visited it, would tread on them. This the Gandharva did and by thus unwittingly insulting S'iva lost his power of moving in the air. He was in consequence caught; when through fear of the King whom he had also offended by the theft of his flowers and with the desire of appeasing S'iva he offered the following supplication to the God.

In making the commentary I have availed myself of that of Jagannātha Chakravarti which is here for the first time printed from a Bengali manuscript in my possession. To his observations which are marked with the initials J. C. I have added my own comments on various matters which the English reader may require to know but which he, writing as a Hindu for Hindus, doubtless considered unnecessary.

Calcutta ARTHUR AVALON
Jan. 3, 1916

By the same Author

THE GREAT LIBERATION

(MAHA NIRVANA TANTRA)

Sanskrit Text, English Translation and Commentary

CONTENTS

"It seems as if the World-Mother has again willed it and has again desired to manifest Her Power so that Arthur Avalon is studying the Tantras and has published so beautiful a version of the Mahānirvaṇa"—*Sahitya.*

3rd Edition (1953) Cloth Bound—Over 1,000 Pages. Price Rs. 30/-

By the same Author

THE SERPENT POWER

The Serpent Power is a description and explanation in fuller detail of the *Serpent Power*—Kuṇdalini S'akti—and the yoga effected through it, a subject occupying a pre-eminent place in the Tantra Shastra. It consists of a translation of two Sanskrit works "Shat Cakra Nirūpaṇa" (description of and investigation into the six bodily centres) and "Pādukā Pañcaka" (Five-fold foot-stool of the Guru). To it is appended a translation from the Sanskrit commentary by Kalicharana. To the translation of both the works is added some further explanatory notes by the author.

This edition contains also the Sanskrit Texts of the works here translated and nine half-tone plates taken from life showing some positions in Kuṇdalini Yoga besides eight original coloured plates of the Chakras. The book is bound in full cloth and gilt.

THE SERPENT POWER

THE GREATNESS OF S'IVA

(MAHIMNASTAVA OF PUṢPADANTA)

I

If praise of Thee by one who knows not the supremacy of Thy greatness [1] be unbecoming
Then even the speech of Brahmā and other Devas regarding Thee is such.[2]
Therefore none should be blamed who speaks
According to the limit of his knowledge,
Oh Hara ! [3] If that be so, then this mine own attempt is blameless.

II

Thy greatness surpasses the powers of mind and speech.
Even S'ruti [4] speaks with awe of Thee,

[1] Which can be known only with the greatest difficulty. Mahimnah param pāram te= Limit of Thy inscrutable greatness. The hymn, it may be noted, has been in some places translated freely but the sense and spirit have been adhered to.

[2] The object of the hymn is praise (Stuti) of the supreme S'iva or Brahman who is greater than all the Devas who have issued from Him.

[3] S'iva. The word is derived from the root H*ri*=to take and the affix *Ach,* for He removes (Harati) all ills. Hara in a higher sense means "He who at the time of Dissolution (Pralaya) withdraws the Universe within Himself". Hari or Viṣṇu comes from the same root with the affix *i* and has the same meaning.

[4] Revelation. The Vedas.

Whom it is unable to portray.[1]
By whom canst Thou be (fitly) praised?
Who knows the number of Thy qualities?
In that which cannot be described,
Whose mind and speech does not fail?

III

Oh Brahman![2] Thy hymn which is the supreme nectar,
By the Guru of the Devas[3]
The creator of sweet words
Is it wonderful to Thee?
Oh Destroyer of Tripura![4]
My mind is bent upon invoking Thee
That I may purify my speech by the recital of Thy
attributes.[5]

[1] That is distinctly and fully as one can point out a jar or a piece of cloth (Ghata-pata). The Brahman, is not the object of any of the four forms of proof, and so it is said of the Devī that She is Etat tad ityanirdeshyā, that is, cannot be said to be this or that. For this or that is the form which the Brahmasvarūpa or Divine Nature, as It is in Itself transcends though manifesting Itself through them (Tris'atī Comm., V, 34). For variant interpretations see note to text.

We know enough to affirm the existence of the Self though as long as we are phenomenal Jīvas we can neither realise Its Nature nor describe It by words which are merely instruments of that dualistic experience which the divine Nature by its definition transcends. As the Brahman's real Self or Nature (Svarūpa) is indescribable Puṣpadanta prays to Him as with form (Sākāra).

[2] Brahman=S'iva.

[3] Bṛhaspati. The Guru of the Devas is the receptacle of all Wisdom and Learning. His Hymns though wonderful to others is not so to S'iva.

[4] S'iva who is so called, as some say, because he was the destroyer of the Asura (Demonic Spirit) Tripura or more correctly because He destroyed the Tripura or three cities of the Asuras. These were built of gold, silver and iron by Maya. Protected by these the Asuras used to oppress all believers.

[5] So in the hymn to Bhuvanes'varī in the Tantrasāra it is said, "Oh Mother by hymning Thy praise I purify my speech." See p. 29, "Hymns to the Goddess" by A. and E. Avalon.

IV

Thy power it is of which the Vedas speak,
Displayed in threefold form according to distinction of qualities.[1]
It creates, maintains and destroys the universe[2]
And yet oh Giver of Blessings!
There be some fools[3] who would oppose Thee
In ways pleasing to the bad but hateful to the good.

V

They ask such questions as:
That Creator of yours why and how does He create the three worlds?[4]

---

[1] That is the three Guṇas, Sattva, Rajas and Tamas the qualities of manifestation, action, and veiling.

[2] The Rajoguṇa prevails in Creation, the Sattvaguṇa in Maintenance and the Tamoguṇa in Dissolution. Through His three bodies, Brahmā, Viṣṇu and Rudra, He creates, maintains and destroys.

[3] According to the commentator, Jagannātha Cakravarti (cited as J. C.), the Mīmāṁsakas (Nāstika Mīmāṁsaka) who attribute all action to the power of Karma are here referred to. As the Commentator on the Tris'atī says "Adṛṣṭa is the cause which gives fruits appearing in the future, of past acts. This is the opinion of the 'Lordless' Mīmāṁsā. Kṛtānāṃ karmaṇāṃ kālāntara-bhāviphala-pradāne adṛṣṭam kāraṇam iti anīs'hvara-mīmāṁsakādi-matam": to which he replies "Not so, because Adṛṣṭa which is an unconscious thing is not to be understood as giving fruit of action which is done by intelligence only" (Jaḍānāṃ sūkṣmānāṃ adṛṭānāṃ cetana-dharma-karmaphala-pradānasāmarthyāyogāt). Adṛṣṭa is instrumental cause (Nimitta-kāraṇa). There is however a conscious Director of Karma who gives fruit according to Adṛṣṭa and He is God.

[4] Such men (the Pratyakṣavādins) talk in terms of human action which they alone see, know and recognise. In such a case it is said that there is first Iṣṭasādhanatājñānaṃ "purpose-serving knowledge" that is knowledge that the proposed act will serve the intention; secondly Pravṛtti or tendency to action; and thirdly Kṛtisādhyatvajñānaṃ "effort-accomplishable knowledge" or the consideration whether that can be done which is followed by action. It is objected if He has not Pravṛtti and so forth, How can he create the three worlds that is Bhūḥ, Bhuvaḥ and Svarloka (J. C.).

What form does He assume?[1]
What means does He use?
What materials does He employ?[2]
From what does He take support?[3]
Such wicked questioning, so ignorant of Thine unimagined greatness,[4]
Leads some senseless men to talk for the delusion of the world.

VI

But is it possible[5] that the worlds with all their parts[6] are uncreate?
Can the universe be without a Supporter of it?
Who else but God creates the world?[7]
Oh Lord of the Immortals!
Such men have doubts concerning Thee because of their folly.

---

[1] For possession of body is asserted to be necessary for action and at Pralaya (Dissolution) body disappears and according to the objector only atomic substance (Paramāṇu) remains (J. C.)

[2] Referring to instrumental and material causes such as in the first case the thread, wheel and stick of the potter and in the second the earth with which the pot is made.

[3] A potter for instance must take his seat on something.

[4] The answer to all this talk is that it is His play (Līlā). It is His nature. It is the "Godness" of God (Etad eva Is'varasya Is'varatvaṁ), that is, He can do all this without being bound by human limitations which if they existed would destroy His Godhead. (J. C.)

[5] He now in answer to the objections of the previous verse gives proof of the existence of God.

[6] It is only the formless without parts which is uncreated as J. C. says Nirākārasyaivājanyatvāt. All things with parts (Sāvayava) are born or created. The universe, therefore, which has parts is created.

[7] But then it is said assuming that they are created what is the proof that it is your God who is the creator? To which the answer is who else but God can create. We are not dealing with some fractional things but with the whole universe with its fourteen worlds. He, who can do this, must have knowledge of the "three times",—Past, Present and Future and must be of an almighty power. Such an one is God.

VII

Though the ways differ which are spoken of in the three-
fold Veda[1]
Sāṁkhya,[2] Yogashāstra,[3] the doctrine of Pas'upati[4] and
Vaiṣṇava S'āstra[5];
Though some take this and others that to be the better
And followers of the various paths both direct and
indirect[6] dispute,
Yet Thou alone art the goal of all
As is the ocean of every river.[7]

VIII

Oh Giver of Boons!
A great bull, a wooden staff,[8] an axe, a tiger skin, ashes,[9]
snakes and a skull,

[1] Trayī that is Ṛk, Yajus and Sāma. (J. C.) The Karmakāṇḍa of the Vedas deals with ritual action (Karma) and Sakāmadharma. The Upaniṣads preach Dhyāna of the Cinmātra Brahma, Niṣkāma Dharma and the attainment of Mokṣa through Jñāna.

[2] Kapila says that we must first enjoy and then relinquish enjoyment attaining Mokṣa through Vivekajñāna on which is realised the difference between Prakṛti and Puruṣa. This Tattvajñāna destroys Karma. As it is elsewhere said first Bhoga and then Yoga.

[3] Which preaches Mukti through Samādhi.

[4] That is the doctrine of S'iva according to the five Āṁnāyas. There is no difference between Īshvara and Mokṣa. Non-dualistic Tattvajñāna is Mokṣa.

[5] Such as the Nāradapāñcarātra, Vaiṣṇava doctrine which treats of Pradyumna, Aniruddha, Saṁkarṣaṇa, and Vāsudeva.

[6] *lit.* "curved and straight".

[7] Having in the previous verse replied to those who are "not towards God" (Bhagavadvimukhān) the Hymnist in this verse speaks of the different ways by which He may be reached. Though the ways may differ their end is the same namely the same Unity so variously sought.

[8] The bull is His carrier. The wooden staff is the support of the Yogī on which he rests his hands at the time of meditation or a piece of wood from the funeral pyre (J. C.)

The colour of Shiva as well as that of the Bull is white. His throat is dark blue encircled by a serpent; His hair of a light reddish colour thickly matted together and gathered over his head in the manner of ascetics.

[9] With which he is covered. "Of whose naked body ashes are the adornment only." Mahānirvāṇa Tantra, ch. I. V. 8.

These be Thy chief possessions and adornments[1]
Varied is the wealth of other Devas[2],
But Thou careth not for these
Which Thou with but a turn of Thine eye,
Hast on them bestowed
The mirage of worldly things does not delude Him
Whose enjoyment is with the Self.[3]

IX

One says[4] that all is permanent[5]
Another that all is fleeting[6]

---

[1] Having praised the Formless the hymnist now chants Him with form, saying "You look but a poor being with all these simple and common things. But this is Thy wish. But Thou could'st have whatever Thou wisheth", namely, such wealth as other Devas have. Simplicity is the mark of the truly great.

[2] Ṛddhi such as the Kaustubha gem, Cakrā, S'aṁkha, Padma and Gadā of Viṣṇu; the crown of Brahmā; the ærial car (Vimāna), the city Amarāvati, the garden Nandana, the elephant Airāvata, the horse Uccais'ravās of Indra and so forth.

[3] Not the limited self (Jīva) that is Caitanyarūpa with the Upādhi Ajñāna but the Brahman who exists in and as the substance of and moves all things as Antaryāmin. Yah sarveṣu bhūteṣu tiṣṭan yah sarvāṇi bhūtāni antaro yamayati. Bṛhad.-Up., 3—7. The Jīva exists as such because he identifies himself with the forms which are produced by the Māyā S'akti of the Brahman. The knower of the Self is not so deluded "Knowing which, oh Pāṇḍava, thou wilt not again be deluded". Yaj jñātvā na punar moham evam yāsyasi Pāṇḍava—Bhagavad-Gīta, IV, 35.

[4] Having dealt with the Nirguṇa and Saguṇa Brahman he proceeds to deal with the variety of philosophical opinion.

[5] Referring to Kapila who says that all is permanent as Puruṣa-Prakṛti with the two states of appearance and disappearance. According to Sāṁkhya both Cause (Kāraṇa) and Effect (Kārya) are real (Sat) for Kārya is nothing but a transformation (Vikṛti) of Kāraṇa (Prakṛti). In Vedānta Kāraṇa is Sat and Kārya, Asat (unreal).

[6] The doctrine of those Buddhists whose psychology is alleged to find no place for the enduring unity of metaphysic which is the Ātmā. Udayanācārya says that the Buddhists allege that Buddhi or the psychic consciousness is Cetana (in-itself conscious) and not dependent for its apparent consciousness on the enduring Ātmā and that hence the followers

And yet another teaches that of the world and its various
. elements
Some things are fleeting and others ever endure,[1]
But Oh Destroyer of Tripura ![2]
Though the multitude of doctrines bewilder me,
I am not ashamed to pray to Thee,
For my tongue cannot be restrained.[3]

X

In order to measure Thy greatness[4] (which is Light and
Fire[5]),
Of Thee who art embodied of Fire,
Viriñci[6] went upwards and Hari[7] downwards

---

of this doctrine are called Buddhists. So the Sarvāstivāda or Kṣaṇikavāda is said to have taught that all is momentary. When a thing is destroyed another identical one is immediately created. In this way the ever changing course of the world seems unchanging like a stream of water in which the water is always changing yet it appears as if the same water is passing through the bed of the river although in fact it is not so. According to the Sensationalists (Vijñānavāda) what is true is sensation which is momentary. According to the Nihilists (Sarvashūnyavāda) the world is like the fleeting objects seen in dream.

[1] The Vais'eṣika and Nyāya Darśanas which say that Ākāśa, Kāla, Paramāṇu, Dik and Ātmā are permanent (Nitya) and the rest are not (Anitya).

[2] See p. 2, note 4.

[3] It is not necessary to know all this. Whatever be Nitya or Anitya matters not. What does matter is that I can pray to Thee from the promptings of a heart full of devotion to Thee. Let the doctors dispute, the course of piety is straight, certain and sure.

[4] According to past traditions (Purā kila as it is said in Sanskrit or in ancient time as we should say) Brahmā and Viṣṇu were one day disputing which of the two were the greater. S'iva then to humble their vanity appeared in the form of a fiery Liṁga which they set out to measure. Their failure to do this made them humble seeing that they, great though they be, were nothing in the presence of the Supreme.

[5] *Lit.* which is a Mass of Fire.

[6] Brahmā. Viriñci comes from the prefix *Vi* indicating various kinds of beings, *Rac* to make or create and the affix *In* in active voice, for He is the aspect of the Trinity (Trimūrti) which creates.

[7] Viṣṇu.

Yet they failed to measure Thee.
But oh Girīs'a![1]
When they prayed to Thee with strength of faith and devotion[2]
It was then that Thou did'st appear to them.
How then is it possible that service of Thee can be without fruit?

XI

Though the Ten-headed One[3] had with ease conquered the three worlds[4],
And destroyed all his enemies therein,
His arms still itched for war
(And fresh worlds to conquer)
O Hara! this was done through unshaken devotion to Thee
And the offering of (nine of) his heads to Thy Lotus feet
As though they were themselves a row of Lotuses.

XII

When Rāvaṇa put forth even against Thine own abode on Kailāsa,[5]

[1] A name of S'iva from Giri + S'a "mountain-sleeping". He who was greatly attached to his wife. Girīs'a is from Giri + Īs'a: Lord of the Mountain Kailāsa.

[2] As J. C. says S'raddhā (faith) is mental worship (Mānasikasevā) whilst Bhakti (devotion) is bodily service (Kāyikasevā) for in it there is also bodily action, such as obeisance, kneeling, the folding of the hands in supplicatory prayer and so forth. True service of S'iva must bring forth the appropriate fruit for the worshipper.

[3] Rāvaṇa the Rākṣasa King of Laṅkā, who had ten heads and twenty arms and whom Viṣṇu in his seventh incarnation as Rāma, son of Das'aratha, King of Ayodhyā, came to destroy. Rāvaṇa was a devotee of S'iva. He offered nine of his ten heads in the ecstasy of his devotion to S'iva like other worshippers do flowers.

[4] The upper, earthly and nether worlds.

[5] Mount Kailāsa, the Himālayan abode and paradise of S'iva.

The force of the forest of arms gained through worship of
Thee
Thou did'st but slightly move the tip of Thy toe
(On which he fell and fell)
And stayed not falling even when he reached the nether
worlds.[1]
So, true it is that the wicked forget the benefits they have
received.[2]

XIII

Oh Giver of boons!
No matter of wonder is it,
That Bāṇa[3] who made the three worlds[4] his servant,
Overcame the great dominion of Indra[5]
Since he worshipped Thy feet,
What prosperity is there not for him,
Whose head has bowed to Thee?

---

[1] According to old traditions (Purā kila) Rāvaṇa used to go every day to Mount Kailāsa to worship S'iva. He found this however troublesome and thought to save himself this trouble of a daily journey by carrying off the whole mountain to his abode in Laṅgkā (Ceylon). He began thereupon to pull up the mountain which trembled as he assaulted it. Pārvatī, S'iva's spouse became afraid and embraced Her Husband for safety. S'iva upon this disturbance merely moved his toe and sent Rāvaṇa tumbling down through space to the nether worlds from which he was subsequently raised by S'iva. Though the strength of Rāvaṇa came to him from the Supreme he forgot this through his wicked nature and assaulted the heaven of S'iva.

[2] Upacito Muhyati Khala*h*= (*lit.*) The wicked (Khala*h*) in prosperity (Upacita*h*) loses his senses (Muhyati), that is, forgets the source of his prosperity.

[3] **Bāṇa was eldest son of Valirāja the Asura and had a thousand arms and with all weapons battled with S'ri Kṛṣṇa. Rāvaṇa also conquered Indra.**

[4] **See note 4, p. 8.**

[5] **Svarga (heaven) only was the conquest of Indra who was conquered by the conqueror of all the three worlds including Svarloka.**

XIV

Oh three eyed One![1]
Who from mercy to Devas and Asuras
And fearful of the threatening destruction of the universe,
Did'st swallow poison,[2]
Doth not its blue stain on Thy throat enhance Thy beauty?
Yea! for even a disfigurement is full of grace[3]
In Him who suffers it
When seeking to rid the world of its fears.

XV

Even Smara[4] whose world-conquering arrows[5]
Are never discharged in vain amidst Devas, Asuras[6] and men
When taking Thee to be like any other Deva[7]
Met with death.[8]
It is not good to attack the self-controlled.

[1] S'iva is called Tryambaka because He had a third eye in his forehead which is that of wisdom (Jnānacakṣuh). An esoteric meaning of the term is that He is "the father of the three" that is Brahmā, Viṣṇu and Rudra. See my note to Ch. V, verse 210 and Ch. I, verse 8 of Mahānirvāṇa Tantra.

[2] At the churning of the ocean poison issued which S'iva swallowed to save the world. This caused a blue stain on His throat whence He is called Nīlakāṇṭha.

[3] Dūṣaṇam api bhūṣaṇam.

[4] The Deva of love; Kāma.

[5] With his arrows he stirs up passion in men and women.

[6] Enemies of the Devas.

[7] Though S'iva is greater than any of them.

[8] Smartavyātmā abhūt=*Lit.* 'became a thing to be remembered, a thing of the past'. The Asura Tāraka excluded all the Devas from heaven. They went to Brahmā. He said that as the Asura had acquired his greatness through His grace He could not take it upon Himself to destroy him. For one does not destroy the tree which one has planted with one's own hand. He however suggested a plan in which the aid of Smara was to be invoked, and that was that S'iva Who was given up to Yoga should be

XVI

By the stamping of Thy feet the safety of the earth came
in sudden peril,
By the movement of Thy arms strong like iron rods,
The stars in the ether were scattered,
Lashed by Thy loosened hair the heavens were troubled.[1]
Verily Thou did'st finely dance,

tempted to unite with Pārvatī, of which union a son would be born who would destroy the Asura. Indra asked Kāma to go with his wife Rati and his companion Vasanta (the Spring) to S'iva's abode Mount Kailāsa. On their arrival and under the influence of the three Devas the season of Spring appeared on the mountain to the great surprise of the Ṛṣis there. Kāma standing behind a tree shot an arrow at S'iva in Yoga at the moment that His wife Pārvatī was putting flowers in His hand having done the hermitage service for the day. As Her hand touched His, Kāma let fly his shaft of passion. S'iva feeling of a sudden passion and loss of seed wondered what was it that thus distracted Him from His Yoga and looking round saw Kāma behind a tree. In anger His third eye flashed fire which consumed Kāma to ashes. S'iva's seed was thrown into Fire who unable to retain it threw it into Gaṅgā who in turn threw it into a reed forest where Kārtikeya called the Reed-born (S'ara-janmā) was born. He became the leader of the celestial hosts and the Destroyer of the Asura as Brahmā intended. The hymn points out however that Kāma was wrong in thinking he might play with impunity with S'iva as with any other, for He is the great Deva and the self-controlled. And yet Kāma in part succeeded though at the risk of his own life—so dangerous it is to tempt the self-controlled.

[1] A Rākṣasa having worshipped Brahmā asked Him to grant him the power to destroy the whole world. Brahmā half assenting half unwilling bade him wait some other time. The other Devas hearing this became afraid and went and spoke to S'iva. The latter then danced in order to delay the granting of this boon by Brahmā and to distract the latter and thus to save the world. But his dancing was so mighty that though done to protect the world its very existence was threatened. The meaning of this incident is explained by another. Some Rākṣasas went to the territory of a King and began destroying a village there. The King sent his army against them to protect the villagers. But this same army was a trouble to them with its extortions and so forth. But while the army was a trouble to the villagers yet it did good to the kingdom which was threatened by the Rākṣasas. Such is the nature of things that it is not possible to do good without some accompanying evil. When we look at the whole *sub specie aeternitatis* what we thought to be evil when considered as a fact detached from its surroundings is no longer seen to be such when taken as part of a whole which is working for good. So with the dance of S'iva.

But to trouble the world in order to save it
What mystery is this?[1]

XVII

By[2] the flowing stream in the skies[3]
The white beauty of which is the whiteness of the countless stars which are the foam therein,
And yet seems (as against Thy greatness) a mere drop of water on Thy head,[4]
The world again became an island encircled by a fluid ring.[5]
By this the divine greatness of Thy body may be gauged.

XVIII

When Thou did'st resolve to consume the three cities[6]
The earth was Thy chariot
The sun and the moon its wheels
Indra[7] the charioteer
The Lord of Mountains[8] Thy bow

[1] Vāmaiva vibhutā. S'iva's Vibhutā (Lordliness) is Vāmā (contrary) to what we see in ordinary human actions. The action of the Lord seems full of contradiction as instanced by His troubling the world to save it. See last note.

[2] Now, as J. C. says, the greatness of His body is celebrated.

[3] The celestial Ganges Mandākinī, the Milky Way. The same stream is in the heavens Mandākinī, on earth Gangā and in the nether world Bhogavatī.

[4] Even the heavenly Ganges but a portion of whose waters were sufficient to surround the world appears as a mere drop on S'iva's head.

[5] Dvīpākāraṁ jaladhivalayam=ocean encircled island. Ṛṣi Agastya once drank up all the waters of the world which thus became dried. In order to restore the water so taken the water of the Ganges on S'iva's head fell to earth when the oceans re-appeared.

[6] Tripuratṛṇam—Tripura which is no better than a blade of grass to S'iva. For Tripura, see p. 2, n. 4, *ante*.

[7] Shatadh*ri*ti.

[8] Meru (J. C.).

And Viṣṇu Himself Thy arrow
(And yet why was this) for they were but as grass before Thy power?
With such implements Thou wert but pleased to play,
Thy Lordliness is not dependent on them.[1]

XIX

Oh Destroyer of Tripura![2]
When Hari[3] desired to worship Thy feet with a thousand lotuses.
But found that one was lacking
He plucked out one of His own lotus-like eyes.[4]
This devotion of His assumed the form of His beautiful discus[5]
Which He is ever ready to wield for the salvation of the three worlds.

XX

When the sacrificial rite is accomplished
It is Thou Who givest the fruits thereof to the worshipper
When the ritual act is over.

[1] Why do so much to destroy that which is but grass before Thee? No one uses an axe when a finger nail is sufficient. He could have done it of His mere wish. The will of God is not dependent on anything. He could have done without them but the play of His will selected them as the instruments of His purpose (J. C.).

[2] See p. 2, n. 4, *ante*.

[3] Viṣṇu.

[4] Viṣṇu was wont to worship S'iva daily with a thousand lotuses. Finding one day that a lotus was missing He, rather than break His rule of worship, plucked out His own eye to make up the number of a thousand. For this devotion S'iva gave Him the Sudarshana Cakra or Discus which Viṣṇu always bears. This discus is itself devotion: devotion, as it were, materialised; and this devotion again it is which saves the world and not any mere material instrument. (J. C.).

[5] The Sudars'ana Cakra, see last note.

How can it have effect without prayer to Thee?
Therefore seeing that it is Thou Who art the surety
For the fruit of all rites
Men repose their faith in Veda
And commence all ritual actions with certain hope as to their effects.[1]

XXI

Oh Thou Who art the refuge of all![2]
Dakṣa[3] was diligent and expert of action[4]
Lord of sacrifices and creatures;[5]
The priests of his sacrifice were Ṛṣis,[6]
And Devas were the masters of the rites,[7]
Nathless Thou, Who givest fruit to all sacrifices,

---

[1] Here the author refers to the fruit of rites. How can a Yajña (sacrifice) which is mere action (Yāgas tu kriyā) give of itself fruit. It arises, exists and is gone (Utpattināsha-dharmayogāt anityah): that is, it is not permanent on account of its being connected with coming into existence and dissolution. Moreover the action (Karma) is here and now but the fruit follows at another time, place and region. It is therefore Shiva and not the Karma which produces the fruit (J. C.)

In this way also the Mīmāṁsakas are refuted though they seek to meet the difficulty by saying that ritual Karma produces Apūrva which exists up to the time of giving and is the giver of fruit. See *ante*, p. 3, n. 3.

[2] Here the Hymnist points out that without prayer (Ārādhana) to the supreme Puruṣa all ritual action is futile.

[3] Dakṣa—father-in-law of S'iva who prepared the great sacrifice known as Dakṣayajna to which however out of slight to Shiva he did not invite Him. S'iva's spouse Pārvatī hearing Her husband abused by Her father yielded up Her life on which S'iva came and destroyed the sacrifice.

[4] Kriyādakṣa.

[5] Kratupati; Tanu-bhṛtām adhīsha*h*.

[6] Seers such as Bhṛgu and others.

[7] Sadasya: that is, the Vidhidars'in or inspector of rites; generally a Brāhmaṇa, who overlooks the carrying out of the rite by the other priests and sees that everything is faultlessly done. In the present case so magnificent was the sacrifice that in lieu of the ordinary Brāhmaṇas, Ṛṣis and Devas were the priests and masters of ceremonies respectively.

Didst destroy his :[1]
For the sacrifice of one, who lacks faith in Thee,
Bears fruit of evil only.

XXII

When the Lord of Creatures[2] overcome by sudden desire[3]
For His own daughter[4]
So urgently desired to possess her[5]
That He changed into a stag
As she fled from Him in the form of a hind,[6]
Thou did'st (in anger) bend Thy bow againt Him
As He sped in fear to the heavenly spaces;[7]

---

[1] For Dakṣa carried out his sacrifices in slight of S'iva. Lack of faith makes all offerings ineffective.

[2] Brahmā.

[3] Here, Brahmā is represented as being subject to the greatest of the passions of His creation but S'iva Whose praise is sung is the self-controlled Who is free of it. Brahmā is associated with the Rajo Guṇa which is the cause of desire—the passion of mankind generally is shown in its collective unit, Brahmā being treated as the Samaṣṭi of mankind. Rajo-Guṇa acts by way of passion, and is here displayed in the acts of the Devatā presiding over it. The incident is referred to in Liṅga Purāṇa and in Kāli Purāṇa though in the latter with some variance. In the seventh century A.D. Kumārila in his Tantravārtika (p. 189 Trans.) explains the incident symbolically as follows :

"The word Prajāpati means one who protects all creatures; as such it can be taken as a name of the sun; and it is an ordinary fact that towards the end of night the sun touches the dawn; as the early dawn is brought about by the sun it is spoken of as his daughter; and it is the following of sun after dawn that has been described as Prajāpati running after his daughter."

[4] Saṁdhyā = the dawn.

[5] Riramayiṣum: indicating the intensity and urgency of His longing.

[6] She in fear of Him changed into a hind whereupon not to be thwarted He changed into a stag.

[7] According to Mārkaṇḍeya Purāṇa when pierced by an arrow He was changed into a star.

And, Oh Lord! the force[1] of Thy hunter's hand
Has even now not released Him.[2]

XXIII

Oh Destroyer of Tripura![3]
Devī saw him of the flowery bow[4]
Burnt to ashes of a sudden before Her very eyes[5]
Like, as it were, some mere blade of grass
When he thought to accomplish his design by the aid of
    Her beauty.[6]
If even Devī after seeing all this
Yet thinks Thee to be uxorious[7]
Because Thou and She art each the half of one body.[8]
Then indeed must youthful women be deceived[9]
Oh Thou Who art self-controlled and the grantor of
    Blessings.

[1] Rabhasa when used in the masculine gender means attachment, effort, love; but in the neuter = force (Byādi Dict.).

[2] S'iva is represented as holding Paras'u (axe), Mṛga (deer) and making with the other two hands the Vara and Abhaya Mudrās. The deer here is Brahmā as above described. S'iva is thus so powerful that even Brahmā is under His subjection, and having captured Him, He has not even up to now released Him. The Hunter holds to what He has got. He is the Giver of bad fruits to those who do bad things.

[3] See note 4, *ante*, p. 2.

[4] Kaṁdarpa or Kāma, Deva of love.

[5] see p. 10, note 8.

[6] His design was to get S'iva to unite with the Devī for the begetting of Kārtikeya. This he thought to do by tempting S'iva with Her womanly beauty. See p. 10.

[7] Strai*n*ang. Here the notion that He is uxorious because He has a spouse is refuted.

[8] Dehārddhagha*t*anāt: "On account of combination of half a body." Male and female are but halves of one whole as Plato also taught. (See II Ch. of the Kumārasaṁbhavam.)

[9] If Pārvatī does not understand S'iva's nature how can ordinary woman folk be expected to do so.

XXIV

Oh Destroyer of Smara![1]
The burning ground is Thy field of play,
Thy companions are Pis'ācas,[2]
Besmeared art Thou with the ashes of the funeral pyre
Thy garland is a string of skulls;
Let even Thy name and nature appear inauspicious
Yet, Oh Giver of Blessings!
To them who meditate on Thee they are supremely auspicious.[3]

XXV

Thou art the great Truth, beyond all words,
On Which the self-controlled deeply meditate,[4]
Fixing their thought abstracted from all outward things
In the manner ordained by Yoga,
Restraining their breath,[5]
Their hairs erect (with joy),
Their eyes filled with tears of joy[6]
Immersed, as it were, in a lake of the nectar of delight.

---

[1] The God of love, v: 15, *ante*, p. 10.

[2] Inferior spirits generally of an unclean nature. S'iva befriends all.

[3] An ordinary man who is attached to such inauspicious things is blamed. But here His extraordinary character is expressed. Nothing is inauspicious to Īs'vara. The worshipper has nothing to do with this. However inauspicious these things appear to him to be, let him remember that S'iva is ever auspicious to those who worship Him. (J. C.) It is only to the Jīva bound in separateness that some things are auspicious and others inauspicious. All such terms involve relativity. Around the Supreme all things are gathered in their natural order.

[4] Here he speaks of the oneness of S'iva with the Parabrahman Who is the inner Tattva (Antastattvam) and hymns Him as such.

[5] By Pūraka, Recaka, Kumbhaka.

[6] Blissful tears as it is commonly said—Ānandās'ru.

XXVI

Thou art Sun, Moon, Air and Fire
Water, Ether, Earth and the Sacrificer too,[1]
By such words did the ancients seek to define and limit
Thee[2]
But we ourselves do not know that which Thou art not.[3]

XXVII

Oh Giver of Refuge!
The Mantra Oṁ[4] with its three letters A, U and M

---

[1] Ātmā: according to Yogavāṣiṣṭa, Yajamāna is so called.

[2] The verse deals with S'iva's eight forms called Aṣṭamūrti. Is'āna (Sun), Mahādeva (Moon), Ugra (Air), Rudra (Fire), Bhava (Water), Bhīma (Ether), S'arva (Earth), and Pas'upati (Yajamāna the sacrificer here called Ātmā).

[3] The ancients (it is here suggested) were unable, as we too are, to conceive the Formless and so conceived of and described S'iva with form as limited intelligence must do. But here eight forms only are given. But there is no form which is not His. Brahman is not the forms which are but finite creatures of His infinite power (S'akti) but is in them as their inmost Self (Pratyagātmā) and Witness (Sākṣī), that is as Knower. It is That, the object of which (as S'aṁkara says) is all the forms ofr knowledge (Sarve pratyayāh viṣaye bhavanti yasya) which is the Knowe- in all cognitions and the Seer in them all as the power of Conscious-ness in-itself (Cicchakti-svarūpa-mātra*h*). Objects (Rūpa) and ideas of objects (Nāma) are the constituents of our differentiated knowledge which is underlain by the undifferenced Blissful consciousness which is true Being or S'iva Himself.

A great sage has put this shortly as thus:

Asti bhāti priyam rūpam nāma cetyams'apañcakam,
Ādyam trayam brahmarūpam jagadrūpam tato dvayam.

Being, radiance, bliss, name, form—these are the five parts or aspects. The first three are the forms of the Brahman. The other two belong to the world (Jagat).

[4] Here he speaks of the great Mantra Oṁ, which is comprised of the letters A and U and M; the first two coalescing by Saṁdhi into O. Its greatness exists both in its wholeness (Oṁ) and the parts which constitute it (samastavyastatayā). It is the mystic (Guhya) syllable of which Manu says! that he who knows its sense knows the Veda (xi, 266). Within it as

Describes Thee collectively and in each its parts[1]
It signifieth
The three Vedas[2]
The three worlds[3]
The three states of consciousness[4]
The three Devas[5]
And the (transcending) fourth state[6] which is Thine,
Encompassed with most subtle Sound.[7]

the first and last is all sound and from it proceed all the seed-mantras (Vījas) of the Tantra. The Praṇava (word of praise) or Oṁ stands for the Brahman and the Vīja Mantras for the various Saguṇarūpa or forms with attributes of the different Devatās.

[1] See last note.

[2] A=Ṛk; U=Yajus; M=Sāman. In this verse the triads of Oṁ are alone referred to but there are Tetrads, Pentads, etc. See my Introduction Prapañcasāra Tantra.

[3] A=Svarga; U=Marttya; M=Pātāla. In the first or Heaven are the Devas in whom the Sattvaguṇa which, as the Sāṁkhyatattva-kaumudī says, is "light (*i.e.*, not heavy) manifestation and desired" (Sattvam laghu prakās'akamiṣṭam). All happiness, kindness, well-being are the effects of this Guṇa. In the second or mortal world there are the contraries: righteousness (Dharma) and unrighteousness (Adharma) for men are dharmādharmayukta: virtue (Pūṇya) and sin (Pāpa) for Rajoguṇa here predominates; and from the third or nether world the gates of which are protected by serpents issue the Asuras and other manifestations of the dark Tamoguṇa.

[4] Waking (Jāgrat), dreaming (Svapna) and dreamless sleep (Suṣupti). See Introduction to my "Six Centres and the Serpent Power". Consciousness itself is Being which is permanent without states; but there appear to be states owing to the reflection of consciousness on the associated unconscious changing forms.

[5] A=Brahmā; U=Viṣṇu; M=Rudra.

[6] Turīya derived from Catur (four) and Ca which the Vedāntasāra defines to be Brahman without Upādhi (Yadanupahitam caitanyam tat turīyam iti ucyate) and which as S'ruti says, is S'āntam (peace), S'ivam (good), Advaitam (non-duality) and, as Sāyaṇa says, the Deliverer (Tāraka). Brahman is Trayī, that is, has a threefold aspect, in the three Devas, with their three Guṇas, Rajas, Sattva, Tamas. This aspect is represented by each of the three letters of which the Mantra is composed. But the supreme unconditioned fourth state both includes and transcends all. It is the indescribable Turīyam Tejas which the whole Mantra indicates.

[7] The supreme subject matter (Pratipādyam) of the Mantra is environed by subtle "Sound" (Sūkṣmanāda) its emanating activities. None can approach thereto save through a knowledge of Bindu, Nāda, etc. See my work last cited.

XXVIII

Bhava, S'arva, Rudra, Pas'upati
Ugra, Mahān, Bhīma, Īs'āna [1]
In each of these names is Mahādeva and S'ruti
To these precious names do I too offer my salutation.

XXIX

Reverence [2] to Thee, Who art near (to those who serve Thee) [3]
And yet art far (from those who are heedless of Thee); [4]
Reverence to Thee, Oh Destroyer of Smara! [5]
Who art both the minutest of the minute [6]
And yet the greatest of the great [7]

[1] See v. 26, *ante* notes; that is S'iva or Mahādeva in His eight forms, as Water, Earth, Fire, the Sacrificer, Air, Moon, Ether and Sun. The eight names are different aspects of the one Great Deva and based on S'ruti or Revelation.

[2] The verse now deals as J. C. says with His apparently contradictory aspects though He is the one unchanging unity in all.

[3] Also as J. C. says because He is our inner Ātmā and ever guides, counsels and protects us. The words in the text are Nediṣṭa (= very near) and Daviṣṭa (= very far).

[4] Or because He is unperceivable beyond mind and speech (J. C.)

[5] V. 15, *ante*, p. 10.

[6] The Brahman is not bound by and transcends all forms whether gross or subtle. The form or non-self is determined and must of nescessity remain such as it is serving the same purpose at all times and under all circumstances. But Consciousness or the Self is free to lend at Its choice relative existence to all or any as the objects of Its knowledge. The Jīva is bound by the form in so far as he identifies himself with it. The Knower being free of such error can assume any form great or small equally because they do not affect the knowing. Therefore is Brahman called the greatest of the great, and the smallest of the small because He is completely free to take any form such, as here, the atomic (the Paramāṇu).

[7] His body is huge manifesting in the great mountains and waters, the earth, the universes and the infinite spaces in which they revolve (J. C.). As Upaniṣad say Aṅoraṇīyān mahato mahīyān,—" more minute than the atom; greatest of the great ".

Reverence to Thee, Oh Three-Eyed One![1]
Who art ancient[2]
And yet very youthful[3]
Reverence to Thee, Who art all things
And art yet beyond all things[4]

XXX

Reverence and again reverence to Bhava[5]
Who with the active quality[6] creates the universe
Reverence and again reverence to Mṛḍa[7]
Who with the quality of manifestation[8] (preserves and) gives happiness to men
Reverence and again reverence to Hara[K]
Who with the quality which veils destroys the universe

---

[1] For he has the third or central eye of wisdom (Jñānacakṣus) or because He is Father of the Three (Trimūrti).

[2] He was before all things (J. C.) the "Ancient of Days".

[3] For He knows not old age and infirmity, but is ever fully strong and capable of all work (J.C.) In this connection may be cited a couplet addressed to the Devī:

Ādyā'pyaśeṣajagatām navayauvanā'si
Nagādhirāja-tanayā' pyatikomalā'si.

'Though the first of all in the endless Universe yet Thou art in the first bloom of Thy youth—although the daughter of the King of Mountains yet art Thou very soft (*i.e.*, full of compassion).'

[4] Visible and invisible. He is not only immanent in the worlds, but transcends them. It cannot be too often repeated that Indian doctrine is not pantheistic in the ordinarily understood western meaning of that term. Brahman in Itself (Svarūpa) is not the form though It exists both *realiter* and *effective* in it but is as Śaṁkara says "the infinite peace, the undual Bhūmā apart from all name and form." It is as the verse says beyond all things that is beyond all categories of time, space and causality and is the "Absolute" only in the sense of a perfectly unrelated and independent self-identity and not in the Hegelian sense of the highest concrete or monadic synthesis of unity in difference. ✓

[5] Here the Supreme S'iva in His aspect as the creator Brahmā.

[6] Rajoguṇa, Sattvaguṇa, Tamoguṇa: lit. "with the aid chiefly of the Rajoguṇa" and so with the others. The three Guṇas co-exist but one or other predominate according as the function is creation, maintenance, or absorption respectively in which case Rajas, Sattva, and Tamas have predominant operation.

[7] The Supreme S'iva in His aspect as Viṣṇu, the Viṣṇurūpa, because He pleases and protects all.

[8] The Supreme S'iva in His aspect as the Destroyer Rudra.

Reverence and again reverence to S'iva
Beyond all qualities in His glittering Abode.[1]

XXXI

How great[2] is the difference between my mind
Capable of but little understanding
And subject to sorrows
And Thine everlasting glory
Which surpasses all attributes,
Yet fearful as I am, my devotion has encouraged me
To offer to Thee, Oh Giver of Blessings!
This garland of words at Thy feet.[3]

XXXII

Oh Lord![4] if the Giver of Happiness[5]
Were to write for all time
With a pen made from a branch of the best of all celestial trees[6]
Using the whole earth as Her leaf[7]

[1] Previously he has dealt with the Triguṇātmaka or Saguṇa Brahma and now he salutes S'iva as the Supreme beyond all Guṇas (Nirguṇa) that is as It exists in Itself and before the creation of the worlds composed of the Guṇas which are the manifestation of its Power (S'akti).

[2] Here the Hymnist expresses his humility (J. C.).

[3] The words of the Hymn are compared to an offering of flowers.

[4] In this celebrated verse he sums up what has hitherto been said as to S'iva's greatness.

[5] S'āradā, that is, Sarasvati, Goddess of Wisdom and Learning; for not wealth but knowledge gives happiness.

[6] These are Mandāra, Pārijātā, Saṁtāna, Haricandana, Kalpavṛkṣa. According to J. C. Pārijātā is here meant.

[7] Patram: as we should say, with anachronism, paper.

If the mass of ink equalled the blue mountains and the ocean were the inkpot
Still would it be impossible to express
The fulness of Thy attributes.

XXXIII

Puṣpadanta
The Chief of the Gandharvas[1]
Servant of the Deva of Devas[2] crested with the crescent moon
Having lost his greatness through Mahādeva's[3] wrath
Has made this best of hymns in praise of the greatness of S'iva.

XXXIV

He[4] who having worshipped the Lord of Devas[5]
The Giver both of Heaven and Liberation[6]
With mind intent and folded palms reads this hymn
Will himself be worshipped by Kiṁnaras[7]
And go to S'iva.
This unfailing[8] hymn has been made by Puṣpadanta

---

[1] Devayoni who according to the Viṣṇu Purāṇa were sons of Brahmā "born imbibing melody", celestial musicians and choristers who play and sing at the bauquets of the Devas belonging together with the Apsarās their wives to Indra's heaven.

[2] The "great Deva" a title of S'iva.

[3] See *ante*, introduction.

[4] Here commences the Phalas'loka which follows all hymns and specifies the reward which is to be got by its recitation.

[5] S'iva.

[6] Svarga, that is, heavenly enjoyment which is yet transient and Mokṣa or Liberation which is beyond the sphere of enjoyment and which endures. God gives both as also earthly bliss which is a faint reflection of the glorious Bhūmā or Divine Bliss which is His nature.

[7] Spirits (Devayoni) of that name.

[8] That is in reaching its object. It is always fruitful and efficacious.

XXXV

With him [1] who reads this hymn
Which has issued from the lotus mouth of Puṣpadanta.
And which is the remover of all sins
With him who learns it by heart
Or keeps it in his house [2]
Mahes'a Lord of Creatures is pleased.

(Here ends the Mahimnastava)

---

[1] This verse occurs in the MS. I have used.

[2] Stotreṇa gṛhasthitena. It is a good thing to have sacred books in one's house even if they are not read. For this possession leads to their being read by the owner or others and the work is thus preserved. So it is said "he who has books in his house is a Pandit (learned man",—Granthī bhavati paṇḍitaḥ.

ॐ

श्रीपुष्पदन्तविरचितं

महिम्नस्तोत्रम्

जगन्नाथचक्रवर्तिविरचितया व्याख्यया, सारार्थदीपिकाख्यया व्याख्यया च संवलितम्

पुरा किल काश्यां पुष्पदन्तनामा गन्धर्वराजो राजोद्यानेषु नक्तं प्रतिदिनमेव पुष्पाण्यपहरति स्म। उद्यानपालास्तु प्रातः प्रातः पुष्पाण्यलभमाना राजभीता मनः-पीडामनुभवन्तो गगनचरेण पुष्पाण्यपह्रियन्त इति गणितशास्त्रविशारदद्वारा निर्णीय, उद्यानेषु विश्वेश्वरनिर्माल्यानि विक्षिप्तवन्तः। स तानि पद्भ्यां स्पृष्ट्वा खेचरत्वादिनिज-महिमहीनतया विधुर उद्यानेषु स्थितः। उद्यानपालैस्तु दृष्टो विश्वेश्वरालयं संगोप्य नीतः तन्महिमानं च स्वयमजानन् कथं स्तुयात् इति प्रतिकारेण स्तवाधिकारिता-मात्मनः प्रकाशयन् स्तौति—

महिम्नः पारं ते परमविदुषो यद्यसदृशी
स्तुतिर्ब्रह्मादीनामपि तदवसन्नास्त्वयि गिरः।
अथावाच्यः सर्वः स्वमतिपरिणामावधि गृणन्
ममाप्येष स्तोत्रे हर निरपवादः परिकरः॥ १॥

महिम्न इति। हे **हर!** ते तव महिम्नो महत्त्वस्य परं दुर्ज्ञानविषयमिति **पारं** पर्यवसानं **अविदुषः** अजानतो जनस्य स्तुतिर्यदि त्वयि असदृशी अयोग्या अनुचितेति **यावत्।** तत् तदा ब्रह्मादीनामपि गिरो वाचः त्वयि **अवसन्ना** अयोग्या भवन्तु,

तेषामपि त्वन्महिमपाराज्ञानित्वात् । अथ यद्यपि सर्वेषामेव महिमपाराज्ञानित्वं तथापि सामर्थ्यानुरूपं प्रयाणं विहगस्येति यथा गरुडस्य गतिस्तथा न चटकस्येति किं चटको न गच्छतीतिन्यायार्थसंवादेन सर्वेषामेव सत्त्वानुरूपं स्तवाधिकारित्वं प्रदर्श्य आत्मनो दर्शयति—अथेति । अथशब्दो यद्यर्थे अव्ययत्वात् । यदि स्वमतिपरिणामावधि स्वबुद्धिपरिपाकपर्यन्तं यथा स्यात् तथा गृणन् अर्थात् त्वां स्तुवन्, सर्वो जनो अवाच्योऽनिन्द्यो भवति । तदा ममापि स्तोत्रे स्तवविषये एष परिकर आरम्भः निरपवादः अपवादशून्यो भवतु । ममापि स्वमतिपरिणामावधित्वेन स्तावकत्वात् । अवपूर्वसद्धातोरवसादवृत्तित्वेनैवायोग्यवृत्तित्वमवसादस्य क्रियायामयोग्यत्वात् । "वाच्यः शक्ये च निन्द्ये च वाच्यं स्याद्वचनेऽपि च" इति **मञ्जरी** ।

"आरम्भे च समूहे च भवेत् परिकरः पुमान् ।
सामग्र्यां परिलोके च संभ्रमे सज्जनेऽपि च" इति **व्याडिः** ॥ १ ॥

सारार्थदीपिका

नत्वा वरदमीशानं सृष्टिस्थित्यन्तहेतुकम् ।
महिम्नस्य स्तुतेर्व्याख्यां कुर्वे सारार्थदीपिकाम् ॥

महिम्न इति । हे हर ; शंभो ! ते ; तव, महिम्नः ; महत्त्वस्य ; **परम** ; अत्यर्थम्, पारम् ; अवसानम् । अविदुषः ; अविजानतः पुरुषस्य, स्तुतिः यद्यसदृशी स्यात्, अननुरूपा अयोग्या भवेद्यदि, तत्तर्हि ब्रह्मादीनामपि गिरः ; वाचः, त्वयि विषये **अवसन्नाः** कुण्ठिता भवेयुः । एवं च न केवलमस्माकं स्तुतावनधिकारित्वम् । किंतु ब्रह्मादीनामपि तथैवेत्यर्थः । एवं पूर्वार्धेन सर्वेषां स्तुतावनधिकारित्वं प्रतिपाद्य, उत्तरार्धेनाधिकारित्वं प्रतिपादयन्नाह—अथेति । अथेति पक्षान्तरे, **सर्वः** समस्तोऽपि जनः, **स्वमतिपरिणामावधि** यथा तथेति क्रियाविशेषणम् । स्वस्य मतिः स्वमतिः, तस्याः परिणामः परिपाकः, सोऽवधिः सीमा मर्यादा यस्मिन् कर्मणि तद्यथा भवति तथा, **गृणन्** स्तुवन् **अवाच्यः** ; अनिन्द्यो भवति । निर्दोष एवायमिति मतं यद्येवं तर्हि हे हर दीनार्तिहर **ममापि स्तोत्रे** स्तुतौ **एषः परिकरः** प्रारम्भः **निरपवादः** निर्दोष एवेति वाक्यार्थः ॥ १ ॥

अथ त्वन्महिमपारविषये ब्रह्मादीनामपि कथमज्ञानित्वमित्याह—

अतीतः पन्थानं तव च महिमा वाङ्मनसयो-
रतद्व्यावृत्त्या यं चकितमभिधत्ते श्रुतिरपि ।

स कस्य स्तोतव्यः कतिविधगुणः कस्य विषयः
पदे त्वर्वाचीने पतति न मनः कस्य न वचः ॥ २ ॥

अतीत इत्यादि। चकारो यस्मादर्थे। यस्मात् तव महिमा वाङ्मनसयोः पन्थानम् अतीत अतिक्रान्तवान् वाङ्मनसयोरविषय इति यावत्। गत्यर्थात् कर्तरि क्तः। वाङ्मनसयोरिति धेन्वनडुहादित्वान्निपातः। वाङ्मनोज्ञानाधीनानां ब्रह्मादीनां त्वन्महिमा ज्ञानगोचरो न भवतीति भावः। अथ यदि महिमा ज्ञानगोचरो न भवेत्, तदा वेदेन कथममिहित इत्याह—अतदित्यादि। यं महिमानं श्रुतिरपि वेदोऽपि अतद्व्यावृत्त्या ब्रह्मभिन्नभेदेन घटपटादिरूपेण वाङ्मनोविषयेण चकितं सभयं यथा स्यात्तथा अभिधत्ते कथयति। ब्रह्मभिन्नभेदत्वेन कथितम्, अतः सभयमित्यर्थः। तच्छब्देन ब्रह्माभिधीयते। तथा च गीतायां—

"ओम् तत् सदिति निर्देशो ब्रह्मणस्त्रिविधः स्मृतः।
ब्राह्मणास्तेन वेदाश्च यज्ञाश्च विहिताः पुरा॥" इति॥

न तत् अतत् ब्रह्मभिन्नम्। तस्य व्यावृत्त्या भेदेनेत्यर्थः। यदाह श्रुतिः—"अथ निष्कलो निरञ्जनो निर्भेद्यो यस्यायं प्रपञ्चो महिमा सर्वाधेयत्वेनानुसंधेयः" इति। यद्वा—अतद्व्यावृत्त्या, न विद्यते तस्य महिम्नो व्यावृत्तिर्भेदो यत्र, एतादृशेन प्रपञ्चस्वरूपेण अभिधत्ते। सर्वेषां त्वन्महिमत्वाद्व्यावृत्तिशून्यता। अतो यं महिमानं वेदोऽपि चकितमभिधत्ते। स महिमा कस्य स्तोतव्यः? अनिर्वचनीयत्वात् कस्यापि नेत्यर्थः। अथ सगुणत्वेनैव निर्वचनीयत्वमिति चेदाह—स **कतिविधगुणः**; कतिविधाः किंधर्मावच्छिन्ना गुणा यस्य तस्य निरूपयितुमशक्यत्वात् अनिर्वचनीयत्वमिति। अथ प्रपञ्चस्वरूपेणैव निरूप्यतामित्याह—कस्य विषयः कस्य प्रमाणस्य गोचरः, न कस्यापि प्रत्यक्षादिप्रमाणाविषयत्वेनानिर्वचनीय इति भावः। अथ यदि कस्यापि प्रमाणस्य गोचरो न भवेत्, कथं तदा स्तवारम्भः क्रियत इत्याह—पदे त्विति। **अर्वाचीने पदे**; चन्द्रशेखरादिरूपे साकारे **कस्य मनो न पतति, कस्य वचो न पतति,** साकारस्य वस्तुनः सर्वेषामेव वाङ्मनोविषयत्वात् साकारमेव स्तौमीति भावः॥ २॥

आद्यश्लोकस्य पूर्वार्धेन स्तुतेरनधिकारित्वमुत्तरार्धेनाधिकारित्वं चोक्तम्; इदानीं भगवतो महिम्नस्येन्द्रियातीतत्वप्रख्यापनाय तथाविधश्रुतिवाक्येनाप्यवधारयितुं न शक्य इति

प्रतिपादयन् स्तौति—अतीत इति। हे भगवन्! तव महिमा वाङ्मनसयोः पन्थानम्; मार्गम्, अतीतः अतिक्रान्तः। वाक् च मनश्च वाङ्मनसे "अचतुर—" इत्यादिना समासान्तो निपातः। तयोः वाङ्मनसयोः, यम्; तव महिमानं श्रुतिरपि वेदोऽपि अतद्व्यावृत्त्या चकितम् अभिधत्ते; तन्न भवतीत्यतत् अंततो व्यावृत्तिः पर्युदासः वर्जनम्, तयापि चकितम् सभयं यथा तथा अभिधत्ते ब्रूते। नेदं भवति, इदं भवतीति निर्दिश्य अभिधत्ते। स इत्थंभूतो महिमा कस्य स्तोतव्यः? अपितु न कस्यापीत्यर्थः। तथा कतिविधगुणः; कतिविधाः कतिप्रकाराः गुणाः यस्यासौ कतिविधगुणः, कियन्तो वा गुणा अस्येति येन केनापि ज्ञातुं न शक्यः। कस्य विषयः? कस्य गोचरो भवेत्। अपितु न कस्यापीत्यर्थः। एतेन निर्गुणस्वरूपस्य ते परमार्थस्य रूपज्ञानं कस्यापि नास्तीत्युक्तम्। स्मृतिपुराणोक्तगुणस्वरूपं तु सर्वोऽपि जानातीति वक्तुमाह—पदे त्वित्यादि। अर्वाचीने सृष्टिस्थितिलयमुख्यतया प्राण्यनुग्राहके पदे स्थाने तु कस्य मनः चित्तं न पतति? कस्य वचः वाक् न प्रसरति? अपितु ब्रह्मादेर्मम च सर्वेषामपि मनो वचश्च प्रसरत्येवेत्यर्थः ॥२॥

अथ यद्यपि शिवः साकारावस्थायां स्तुतिविषयः, तथाप्याश्चर्यस्तुतिस्तु तश्चेन्मङ्गलदस्तत्र ब्रह्मादीनामपि स्तुतिर्न तस्याश्चर्यकारिणी किमन्येषामिति प्रतिपादयति—

मधुस्फीता वाचः परमममृतं निर्मितवत-
स्तव ब्रह्मन् किं वागपि सुरगुरोर्विस्मयपदम्।
मम त्वेतां वाणीं गुणकथनपुण्येन भवतः
पुनामीत्यर्थेऽस्मिन् पुरमथन बुद्धिर्व्यवसिता ॥ ३ ॥

मध्विति। हे ब्रह्मन्! हे शिव! सुरगुरोः, बृहस्पतेः, वाक् वाणी मधुस्फीता माध्वीकवन्मधुरापि तव किं विस्मयपदम् आश्चर्यस्थानम्, अपितु नैव। यतस्तव कीदृशस्य वाचो वाक्यतः परमम् उत्कृष्टम् अमृतं पीयूषं निर्मितवतः निर्माणकर्तुः। यस्य वाणी उत्कृष्टा अमृतनिर्माणकारणीभूता तस्य तु कथं मधुवन्मधुरा वागाश्चर्यपदं भविष्यतीति भावः। मधुनः पीयूषस्य उत्कृष्टास्वादजनकत्वादिति भावः। अथ तर्हि यस्य बृहस्पतेरपि वाक् नाश्चर्यपदं तस्य स्तवे ततोऽपि न्यूनो भवान् कथं प्रवर्तत इत्युपहासं जिहीर्षुः स्तवकरणकारणमाह—ममेति। हे पुरमथन! हे पुरारे! भवतो गुणकथनपुण्येन भवद्गुण-

कीर्तनजन्यपुण्येन मम एतां वाणीं गुणरूपां पुनामि पवित्रं करोमि इति कृत्वा अस्मिन्नर्थे स्तवकरणे मम बुद्धिर्व्यवसिता व्यवसायवती उद्युक्ता इत्यर्थः। अत एव हि स्तवे प्रवर्ते इति भावः। "मधु माध्वीकमद्ययोः" इत्यमरः। "स्फीतं प्रफुल्ले मधुरे प्रस्फुटे च नपुंसकम्" इति व्याडिः। "पीयूषममृतं सुधा" इति "विस्मयोद्भुतमाश्चर्यम्" इत्यप्यमरः॥ ३॥

इदानीं माहात्म्यस्य स्तोतुमशक्यत्वेन स्तुवतो यो दोषस्तं परिहर्तुमाह— मधुस्फीता इति। हे ब्रह्मन्! तव सुरगुरोः बृहस्पतेः अपि वाक् वचः विस्मयपदं किम्? आश्चर्यस्थानं भवति किम्? न भवतीत्यर्थः। किं भूतस्य तव? वाचः गिरः निर्मितवतः रचयतः, किं भूता वाचः? मधुस्फीताः; माधुर्यगुणेन युक्ताः। पुनः कथंभूताः? परमममृतम् उत्कृष्टममृतम। अमृतस्वरूपत्वादमृतमित्युपचारः। अस्मदादेर्वाक् किं पुनः? यद्येवं स्तुतिः किमर्थमारभ्यत इत्याशङ्क्याह—मम त्विति। मम बुद्धिस्तु, हे पुरमथन! एतां मदीयां वाणीं भवतः गुणकथनपुण्येन पुनामीत्यस्मिन्नर्थे व्यवसिता कृतोद्यमा॥ ३॥

तवैश्वर्यं यत्तज्जगदुदयरक्षाप्रलयकृ-
त्त्रयीवस्तु व्यस्तं तिसृषु गुणभिन्नासु तनुषु।
अभव्यानामस्मिन् वरद रमणीयामरमणीं
विहन्तुं व्याक्रोशीं विदधत इहैके जडधियः॥ ४॥

तवेति। हे वरद! हे शिव! इह तु भुवने तव यदैश्वर्यं प्रभुत्वं जगतां सृष्टिस्थितिप्रलयकारिरूपं तद्विहन्तुं निरसितुम् एके जडधियः जडबुद्धयः नास्तिकमीमांसकाः व्याक्रोशीं विप्रतिपत्तिं विदधते कुर्वन्ति। अथैश्वर्यस्य विद्यमानत्वे किं प्रमाणमित्याह—ऐश्वर्यं कीदृशम्? त्रयीवस्तु वेदत्रयप्रतिपाद्यम्। अथ एकस्य ऐश्वर्यस्य सृष्टिस्थितिप्रलयानां संबन्धे कर्तृत्वं कथमित्याह— पुनः कीदृशम्? गुणैः सत्त्वरजस्तमोभिर्भिन्नासु भेदं गतासु तिसृषु तनुषु शरीरेषु ब्रह्मविष्णुशिवरूपासु व्यस्तं विभक्तम्। गुणभेदाच्छरीरभेदः तद्भेदे ऐश्वर्यस्यापि भेदो लक्ष्यते, न तु वास्तव इति भावः। अतो ब्रह्मविष्णुशिवशरीरेण जगतां सृष्टिस्थितिप्रलयकारित्वेन वेदत्रयप्रतिपाद्यैश्वर्यनिरासका नास्तिका जडधिय एव। अथ तादृशी व्याक्रोशी सर्वमनोरञ्जिनी न इति प्रतिपादयन्नाह— व्याक्रोशीं कीदृशीम्? अस्मिन् ऐश्वर्यविषये अभव्यानाम्,

अज्ञानिनां रमणीयां मनोरञ्जिनीम्, परमार्थतस्तु अरमणीं कुत्सिताम्। यद्वा अस्मिन् ब्रह्मादिशरीरे अभव्यानाम् असन्मतानां रमणीयाम्। तथा च सर्वा एव देवता मन्त्रमयीति प्रतिपन्नाः केचिन्मीमांसका ईश्वरस्य मूर्तिं न मन्यन्ते, अतस्तेषां ब्रह्मादिशरीरद्वारा जगदुदयादिकार्यैश्वर्ये व्याक्रोशी रमणीयैव, परमार्थतोवेदप्रतिपाद्यत्वात् सा अरमणीया इत्यर्थः। "स्त्रियामृक् सामयजुषी इति वेदास्त्रयस्त्रयी" इत्यमरः। वस्तु अर्थः स एव प्रतिपाद्यम्। "गुणाः सत्त्वं रजस्तमः" इत्यमरः, "आक्रोशी प्रतिपत्तिः स्यादाक्रोशः क्रोध उच्यते" इति च ॥ ४ ॥

आत्मस्तुतेः सावकाशत्वं प्रतिपाद्य, इदानीं ये मीमांसका ईश्वरो नास्तीति वदन्ति तान् निराकर्तुमाह—तवेति। हे वरद! अभयद! तव ऐश्वर्यम् यत् तत् जगदुदयरक्षाप्रलयकृत्; जगतां लोकानाम् उदय उत्पत्तिः, रक्षा परिपालनं, प्रलयो नाशश्चेति द्वन्द्वः, तान् करोतीति तत्कृत्। किं भूतम्? त्रयीवस्तु त्रय्याः वेदत्रय्याः वस्तु प्रतिपाद्यम्। तथा तिसृषु तनुषु मूर्तिषु व्यस्तं विभज्य विक्षिप्तम्। किं भूतासु तनुषु? गुणैः सत्त्वरजस्तमोभिः भिन्नासु पृथग्भूतासु ब्रह्मविष्णुशिवात्मिकासु, इह लोके एके जडधियः ये केचित् जडधियो मन्दबुद्धयः अस्मिन् ऐश्वर्ये व्याक्रोशीं निन्दां विदधते कुर्वते। किं कर्तुम्? विहन्तुं नाशयितुम्। किं भूतां व्याक्रोशीम्? अभव्यानाम्; असताम्, अपुण्यभाजां रमणीयाम्; मनोरमाम्। पुनः किं भूताम्? परमार्थतस्तु ऐश्वर्यादिगुणोपेते त्वयि अरमणीयामशुभामित्यर्थः ॥ ४ ॥

ऐश्वर्यप्रतिपन्नानां मतमुपन्यस्य विप्रतिपत्तिप्रकारं दर्शयन् तामेव निरस्यन् स्तौति—

किमीहः किं कायः स खलु किमुपायस्त्रिभुवनं
किमाधारो धाता सृजति किमुपादान इति च।
अतर्क्यैश्वर्ये त्वय्यनवसरदुःस्थो हतधियः
कुतर्कोऽयं कांश्चिन्मुखरयति मोहाय जगतः ॥ ५ ॥

किमीह इति। हे हर! अयं कुतर्कः कुत्सितः पूर्वपक्षः कांश्चित् हतधियो मायया विनष्टबुद्धीन् वेदविरुद्धवादिनो मीमांसकादीन् मुखरयति वाचालं करोति, तव

पुनर्जगतो मोहाय नान्यत् फलम् । तं कुतर्कमेव निरासयति—यतः कुतर्कः अतर्क्यै अतर्कणीयम् ऐश्वर्य्यं यस्य तादृशि अपरिच्छेद्यविभवे त्वयि अनवसरेण निरवकाशतया बाधित इति हेतुगर्भं विशेषणम् । यतस्त्वयि कुतर्को नावतिष्ठते, अतो जगन्मोहनमात्रं तस्य फलं नान्यदिति भावः । कुतर्कमेवाह—**किमीह** इति । स्वस्वित्युपहासार्थे । वेदविरुद्धवादिनो जनाः वेदार्थपरिनिष्ठितान् प्रति कुतर्काभासेन उपहसन्ति । अथ इष्टसाधनज्ञानशरीरनिमित्तकारणाधारसमवायिकारणरूपसामग्रीकलापमेव सृष्टिकर्तृत्वं, तत्र तव स धाता सृष्टिकर्ता किमीहः सन् त्रिभुवनं सृजति । का ईहा इष्टं यस्य, तस्य किमिष्टं किञ्चिदपि न, इष्टाभावात् इष्टसाधनज्ञानाभावेन प्रवृत्तेरभावात् कथं सृजतीति कुतर्कः । तथा कः कायोऽस्येति किंकायः सन् सृजति । प्रलयमङ्गीकुर्वतां भवतां परमाणुमात्रावशिष्टतया सृष्टेः प्राक्क्षणे कस्यापि शरीरस्याभावात् शरीर-सहकारिसृष्टिकर्तृत्वं बाधितमेवेति भावः । तथा क उपायो निमित्तकारणमस्य यथा घटकर्तुः कुलालस्य दण्डचक्राद्युपायः, तथा सृष्टेः पूर्वं किञ्चिदपि निमित्तकारणं नास्तीति कथं सृजतीति । यत् पुनः परमाणवोऽवशिष्टास्तेऽपि न कारणानि, परमाणूनां कारणत्वानङ्गीकारात् । अभ्युपगमेऽपि निमित्तत्वं नास्त्येवेति समवायित्वात् । तथा क आधारो यस्य किमाधारः यथा मर्कटादीनां सूत्रजालकर्तृत्वे तृणाद्याधारस्य कुलालानां घटकर्तृत्वे तृणाद्याधारस्य सहकारिता तथा सृष्टेः प्राक् कस्यापि वस्तुनः स्थित्यभावे-नाधारस्याभावात् अनाधारस्य धातुः कथमाधारसहकारिसृष्टिकर्तृत्वं संभवतीति भावः । अथ किमुपादानं समवायिकारणं यस्य यथा कपालादिकं घटस्य तथा सृष्टेः प्राग्वस्तु नास्तीति किं समवायिकारणं भवेत् अतस्तदभावात् कथं सृष्टिरिति भावः । परमाणूनां कारणत्वमङ्गीकृत्येदमुक्तं । वस्तुत इष्टसाधनसामग्री ईश्वरस्य सृष्टिकर्तृत्वे सहकारिणी तस्य पुनरतर्कणीयत्वाज्जडधियामेव कुतर्कः, न तु ज्ञानिनाम् । एतदेव ईश्वरस्येश्वरत्वमिष्टादिसामग्रीमन्तरेणापि सृष्टिकर्तृत्वमिति ध्येयम् ॥ ५ ॥

एतामेव व्याक्रोशीं प्रकटयति—**किमिति**। तिसृषु गुणभिन्नासु तनुषु तवैश्वर्यं व्यस्त-मित्यनेन धातृरूपेण सृजति, विष्णुरूपेण पालयति, रुद्ररूपेण हरतीत्युक्तम्; तद् दूषयन्त्याहुः। सः; ईश्वरः धाता भूत्वा ब्रह्मरूपेण त्रिभुवनं सृजति । किमीहः सृजति ? क उपायः सामग्री यस्य स तथोक्तः । कुत्र स्थितः सृजतीत्यर्थः । किमुपादानः सृजति । कार्यं यत्र समवैति, तदुपादानकारणं, यथा घटस्य मृत्पिण्डः, पटस्य

तन्तवः ; तद्वत् लोकनिर्माणे धातुरुपादानं किम् ? उपादानकारणं विना कार्यं न सिद्ध्यतीति भावः । इति अनेन प्रकारेण अयं कुतर्कः जगतां मोहाय भ्रान्तिमुत्पादयितुं कांश्चित् हतधियः पुरुषान् मुखरयति वाचालयति । स तर्कों दुस्थो दुर्लभस्तुच्छ इत्यर्थः । त्वयि विषये तस्य अनवरस एव । किं भूते त्वयि ? अतर्क्यैश्वर्ये ; अतर्क्यमनूह्यमैश्वर्यं यस्य तस्मिन् ॥ ५ ॥

इत्थं प्रतिकूलतर्कं निरस्य ईश्वरसाधकानुमानप्रकारं दर्शयन् स्तौति—

अजन्मानो लोकाः किमवयववन्तोऽपि जगता-
मधिष्ठातारं किं भवविधिरनादृत्य भवति ।
अनीशो वा कुर्याद्भुवनजनने कः परिकरं
यतो मन्दास्त्वां प्रत्यमरवर संशेरत इमे ॥ ६ ॥

अजन्मान इति । हे अमरवर ! हे अमरश्रेष्ठ ! **अवयववन्तोऽपि** ; सावयवादयोऽपि **लोकाः** क्षित्यादयः **किमजन्मानः** ? किं जन्महीनाः । अपि तु जन्या एव, सावयवत्वात् । न हि जन्मव्यतिरेकी सावयवोऽस्ति । निराकारस्यैवाजन्यत्वात् । तेन सावयवत्वेन क्षित्यादेर्जन्यत्वमनुमितमिति भावः । एवं जन्यत्वेनानुमीयमानानां जगतां **भवविधिः** ; जन्मविधानं **किमधिष्ठातारम्** ; कर्तारम् , **अनादृत्य** ; अनपेक्ष्य, किं भवति, अपितु नैव । तथा च वासिष्ठे "कार्यं सकर्तृकं ज्ञेयम्" इति । अथ क्षित्यादयः सावयवा जन्याः सकर्तृकाश्च सन्तु । तत्रेश्वरस्य कर्तृत्वे किं मानमिति निरस्यति—**अनीश** इति । अनीशः ईश्वरादन्यः को जनः **भुवनजनने** ; विश्वोत्पत्तौ, **परिकरम्** ; आरम्भं कुर्यात्, न कोऽपीत्यर्थः । भूतभविष्यद्वर्तमानानभिज्ञानामीश्वरभिन्नानां विचित्रचतुर्दशभुवनरचनासमर्थानां भुवनजननारम्भोऽसंभव एव । अतः हे सर्वज्ञ ! त्वमेव रचयसीति यतस्ते मन्दा मोहयुक्ताः, अतस्त्वां प्रति **संशेरते** अस्ति नास्तीति संशयं कुर्वते । संपूर्वकशीधातोः संशयवृत्तित्वमनेकार्थत्वात् । शेतेरदादेरुडागमः । "लोकस्तु भुवने जने" इत्यमरः । "भवो जन्मनि संसारे प्रकाशे चोद्भवो मतः" इति "आरम्भे च समूहे च भवेत् परिकरः पुमान्" इतिच व्याडिः ॥ ६ ॥

अजन्मान इति। हे अमरवर! अमरश्रेष्ठ! भूधराद्यवयववन्तो हि लोकाः अजन्मानः जन्मरहिताः किम्? न विद्यते जन्म उद्भवो येषां ते अजन्मानः किम? किं शब्द आक्षेपे। योऽवयववान् स जन्मीत्युच्यते। तथाहि सावयवो घटः उत्पत्तिमानेव दृश्यते। भवतूत्पत्तिमान्, एतावता किं लभ्यत इत्याह—जगतामिति। जन्मवतां जगतां लोकानाम्, भवविधिः; उत्पत्तिविधिः, अधिष्ठातारम्; उत्पादकं, कर्तारम्; अनादृत्य; अनपेक्ष्य भवति किम्? यतः यस्मात् कारणात् इमे मन्दाः स्वल्पबुद्धयः मीमांसकाः त्वां प्रति त्वामुद्दिश्य संशेरते संशयं कुर्वते। अतः त्वां प्रति संदेहो न कर्तव्य इति भावः। एतावत्युक्ते किम्? पुनः पूर्वपक्षे। भवत्वधिष्ठाता च, एतावता कथमीश्वरसिद्धिरित्यभिप्रायेणाह—अनीश इति। अनीशो वा; ईश्वरादन्योऽपि वा कुर्यात्। तदपि दूषयति—भुवनेति। भुवनजनने लोकोत्पादने, कः परिकरः समर्थः?॥ ६॥

एवं भगवद्विमुखान् निरस्य सर्वेषामेव प्रस्थानानां भगवत्येव साक्षात् परंपरया च तात्पर्यं प्रकाश्य स्तौति—

त्रयी सांख्यं योगः पशुपतिमतं वैष्णवमिति
प्रभिन्ने प्रस्थाने परमिदमदः पथ्यमिति च।
रुचीनां वैचित्र्यादृजुकुटिलनानापथजुषां
नृणामेको गम्यस्त्वमसि पयसामर्णव इव॥ ७॥

त्रयीति। अथेश्वरप्राप्तिसाधने नानावर्त्म वर्तते। तत्र त्रयी; त्रयो वेदा धर्मब्रह्मप्रतिपादकापौरुषेयप्रमाणवाक्यं वेदः, स एव ऋग्यजुःसामभेदेन त्रयी इत्युच्यते। तेषां मते ध्यानमात्रेणैव ईश्वरो गम्यः। तथा च श्रुतिः; "चिन्मात्रं चिन्तनापेक्षि कार्यं कर्मानुयोगतः" इति। चिन्मात्रं ब्रह्म चिन्तनापेक्षि ध्यानप्राप्यं कार्यं जन्यं शरीरि कर्मानुयोगतः यागाद्यनुष्ठानेन गम्यम्। यथा श्रुत्यन्तरम्; "न कर्मणा न प्रजया न धनेन त्यागेनैके अमृतत्वमानशुः" इति। अत्रेश्वरध्यानमेव ज्ञानं जनयति ततो मोक्षः। अन्यत्तु सांख्यम्; कपिलोक्तं शास्त्रम्, तन्मते तत्त्वज्ञानमेव यावत् कर्म नाशयति, तत एव ईश्वरो गम्यः। तथा च गीतायां;

"ज्ञानाग्निः सर्वकर्माणि भस्मसात् कुरुतेऽर्जुन।
क्षीयन्ते चास्य कर्माणि तस्मिन् दृष्टे परात्मनि॥" इति।

तत्र हि यागादिसाध्यतत्त्वज्ञानमेव मोक्षकारणम् । तथा च कापिले;

"कर्मणा जन्यते ज्ञानं ज्ञानतो मोक्षसाधनम् ।
तदेव ब्रह्मगमनं कर्मयोगेन वर्त्मना ॥" इति ।

अन्यत्तु योगः; अध्यात्मशास्त्रम्, तन्मते भोगेन यावत् कर्म क्षीयते ततः स्वतन्त्रेणैव तत्त्वज्ञानमुत्पद्यते; ततो मोक्षः । तथा च वासिष्ठे;

"नाभुक्तं क्षीयते कर्म कल्पकोटिशतैरपि ।
अवश्यमेव भोक्तव्यं कृतं कर्म शुभाशुभम् ॥
भोगान्ते जायते ज्ञानं स्वतस्ततो विमुञ्चति ।
तस्मात् कर्म न कुर्वीत मोक्षार्थी मोक्षबाधनम् ॥" इति ।

अन्यत्तु पशुपतिमतम्; पाशुपतं शास्त्रं भगवता पशुपतिना पशुपाशविमोक्षणाय, "अथातः पाशुपतं योगविधिं व्याख्यास्यामः" इत्यादि पशुपाशादिपञ्चकान्वितपञ्चाध्यायविरचितम् । एतन्मते तत्त्वज्ञानमेव मोक्षः । न तु कार्यकारणसंबन्धः । तदेव महेश्वर इति तत्त्वज्ञानमोक्षेश्वरनामभेदत्वं प्रतिपादितम् । तथाचोक्तम्;

"व्याचष्टे तारकं ज्ञानं स्वयं देवो महेश्वरः ।
तदेव ब्रह्म विज्ञेयं न च कारणकार्यता ॥" इति ।

एतन्मते ज्ञानिनां नारदादीनां जीवन्मुक्तत्वं साधु । अन्यत्तु वैष्णवम्; विष्णुना प्रणीतं हयशीर्षपाञ्चरात्रादि; तन्मते यागादिसाध्य एव मोक्षः । तथा च;

"आरुरुक्षोर्मुक्तिमार्गे कर्म कारणमुच्यते ।
योगारूढस्य तस्यैव साक्षान्मोक्षो भवेत् स्वयम् ॥" इति ।

एवंप्रकारेण प्रस्थाने दर्शने मते प्रभिन्ने सति एको वदति इदं परम्, एको वदति अदः पथ्यम् इति रुचीनां वैचित्र्यात् इच्छाविशेषाणां नानाप्रकारत्वात् ऋजुकुटिलनानापथजुषां समानवक्रपथवर्तिनां नृणां साक्षात् परंपरया च त्वमेवैको गम्यः । वेदवाक्यानुगृहीतमननरूपपथवर्ती साक्षात् अन्यपथवर्ती परंपरया लभत इत्येव विषयविभागः । यथा पयसां जलानां अर्णवः समुद्रः, यथा ऋजुपथजुषां गङ्गादिजलानां साक्षादर्णवो गम्यः । कुटिलपथजुषां यमुनासरस्वतीजलानां गङ्गादिप्रवेशद्वारा परंपरया समुद्रो गम्यस्तथेति भावः ॥ ७ ॥

त्रयीति। त्रयाणां वेदानां समाहारः त्रयी; असावेको मार्गः; तथा सांख्यम्; कापिलं शास्त्रं पञ्चविंशतितत्त्वोपलक्षितम्; स एको मार्गः; योगः; पातञ्जलादि, अथवा वासिष्ठादिशास्त्रम्, स एको मार्गः; पशुपतिमतम्; शैवागमे नकुलीशसिद्धान्तः, शैवसिद्धान्तः, सोमसिद्धान्तः, पञ्चार्थसिद्धान्तः, कुलसिद्धान्तश्चेति, स एको मार्गः; वैष्णवम्; वैष्णवागमः पाञ्चरात्रादि, स एको मार्गः; इति अनेन प्रकारेण प्रस्थाने प्रभिन्ने नानात्वं गते सति, प्रस्थीयते गम्यते अनेनेति प्रस्थानं मार्गः, तस्मिन् प्रभिन्ने सति इदं परम् उत्तमम्; अदः पथ्यम् हितमित्येवं प्रकारेण, रुचीनाम्; इच्छानाम्, वैचित्र्यात्; भिन्नत्वात्, ऋजुकुटिलनानापथजुषाम्; केचिन्मार्गा ऋजवोऽकुटिलाः, केचिन्मार्गाः कुटिलाः वक्रा इति नानापथजुषाम्; अनेकमार्गसेविनां नृणां मनुष्याणाम्, त्वम् एको गम्यः; प्राप्योऽसि। येन केन वा मार्गेण गच्छतां पयसां जलानाम् अर्णव इव; समुद्र इव, एक एव यथा प्राप्यः तथा त्वमित्यर्थः ॥ ७ ॥

एवं सर्वशास्त्रसंमतनिराकारावस्थं संस्तुत्य भगवतः परमेश्वरस्य साकारावस्थां प्रतिपादयन् स्तौति—

महोक्षः खट्वाङ्गं परशुरजिनं भस्म फणिनः
कपालं चेतीयत्तव वरद तन्त्रोपकरणम्।
सुरास्तां तामृद्धिं दधति तु भवद्भ्रूप्रणिहितां
न हि स्वात्मारामं विषयमृगतृष्णा भ्रमयति ॥ ८ ॥

महोक्ष इति। हे वरद! महोक्षो वृद्धवृषः; खट्वाङ्गं चितिकाष्ठम्; परशुः कुठारः; अजिनं गजव्याघ्रयोश्चर्म; भस्म अङ्गलेपकदग्धकाष्ठादिरूपपांसुः; फणिनः सर्पाः; कपालं मानुषशिरोऽस्थि; तव इयत् एतावत् तन्त्रोपकरणं प्रधानसामग्री। सुरास्तु इन्द्रादयः पुनः, भवद्भ्रूप्रणिहिताम्; तव भ्रूविक्षेपमात्रेण समर्पितां तां तां अनिर्वचनीयां इन्द्रत्वादिरूपाम् ऋद्धिं संपत्तिं दधति धारयन्ति। महोक्षादिसामग्रीदर्शनात् त्वमतिदरिद्रः। तव सेवनया इन्द्रादयो देवाः समृद्धा इति। भेदकस्तुशब्दः। अथ यस्य दृष्टिपातेनैव देवाः समृद्धाः तस्य इयत् तन्त्रोपकरणं कथमित्याह—नहीति। हि यस्मात् आत्मारामं जनं परमेश्वररूपं विषया इन्द्रियार्थाः शब्दस्पर्शरूपरसगन्धाः, त एव मृगतृष्णा मरीचिकावत् मिथ्यारूपा न भ्रमयति न

मोहयति। आत्मनि ब्रह्मण्येव चिदानन्दे आरमते क्रीडति तस्य तव इन्द्रियार्थाः शब्दस्पर्शादिविषया यतो मृगतृष्णादिवन्मिथ्या अतः कथं मोहजनका भविष्यन्ति। अतो बाह्यवस्तुनि अनास्थातः निस्पृहत्वप्रतिपादकमहोक्षाद्युपकरणधारणेन सारूप्याकाङ्क्षिवञ्चनमेव प्रयोजनं मन्यामह इति भावः। "तन्त्रं प्रधाने सिद्धान्ते सूत्रवाये परिच्छदे" इत्यमरः॥ ८॥

महोक्ष इति। महांश्चासौ उक्षा चेति महोक्षः; महाबलीवर्दः। महोक्ष इति "अचतुर—" इति सूत्रेणाकारान्तो निपातः। खट्वाङ्गम्; प्रसिद्धम्, दण्डस्योपरि ब्रह्मकपालं खट्वाङ्गमुच्यते। परशुः; कुठारः, अजिनम्; चर्म, भस्म; भसितम्, फणिनः; सर्पाः, कपालम्; शिरोऽस्थि, चकारः समुच्चयः। इतिशब्दोऽवधारणे। इयत्; एतावदेव, हे वरद! अभयवरद! तव तन्त्रोपकरणम्; उपक्रियते अनेनेत्युपकरणम्, उपकारकमित्यर्थः। तन्त्ररूपेण प्रपञ्चरूपेण स्थितमुपकरणमेतावदेव। सुरास्तु; इन्द्रादयः पुनः, तां तामृद्धिम्; तां तां संपदम्, दधति; धारयन्ति। किं भूताम्? भवद्भ्रूप्रणिहिताम्; भवतः तव भ्रूप्रणिहितां भ्रूक्षेपमात्रेण उपनीताम्, भ्रूदत्तामित्यर्थः। यद्येवमेतावती शक्तिरस्ति, तर्हि भवान् कथं स्वयमेव नाभजदित्याह—न हीत्यादि। हि यस्मात्कारणात्, स्वात्मारामम्; स्वात्मनि स्वकीयात्मनि, आरमते क्रीडतीत्यात्मारामं भगवन्तं, विषयमृगतृष्णा न भ्रमयति; न चालयति। इन्द्रियग्राह्यार्थः शब्दादिर्विषयः, स एव मृगतृष्णा मरीचिका। एतदुक्तं भवति—भगवान् परमयोगी विषयैर्न बाध्यत इति॥ ८॥

एवं परमेश्वरस्य सगुणनिर्गुणभावं प्रकाश्य संप्रति स्तुतेर्नानाप्रकारं दर्शयन् स्तौति—

ध्रुवं कश्चित् सर्वं सकलमपरस्त्वध्रुवमिदं
परो ध्रौव्याध्रौव्ये जगति गदति व्यस्तविषये।
समस्तेऽप्येतस्मिन् पुरमथन तैर्विस्मित इव
स्तुवञ्जिह्रेमि त्वां न खलु ननु धृष्टा मुखरता॥ ९॥

ध्रुवमिति। हे पुरमथन! हे हर! कश्चित् सांख्यमतानुसारी सर्वं जगत् ध्रुवं नित्यं गदति। जगत् सदेवाभिव्यक्तम्; न चासदुत्पद्यते; न च सद्विनश्यति;

उत्पत्तिविनाशयोराविर्भावतिरोभावरूपत्वादित्येकः पक्षः। अपरस्तु कश्चित् सकलं जगत् अध्रुवमनित्यं क्षणिकमिति गदति। न ह्यसतः स्थिरत्वं संभवति। अर्थक्रियाकारित्वं हि सत्त्वम्, ततश्चैकस्मिन्नेव क्षणे अर्थक्रियासमाप्तेः; उक्तलक्षणेऽर्थक्रियाकारित्वाभावात् सत्त्वमेवेति द्वितीयः पक्षः। परो नैयायिकः समस्तेऽप्येतस्मिन् जगति ध्रौव्याध्रौव्ये नित्यत्वानित्यत्वे व्यस्तविषये विभक्तधर्मे गदति। आकाशादि नित्यम्, अनित्यं घटपटादि; अनित्यानामुत्पत्तिविनाशौ स्तः। न तु नित्यानामिति। तैर्नित्यानित्यतदुभयप्रकारैस्त्वां स्तुवन् विस्मित इव जातचमत्कार इव न जिह्नेमि नाहं लज्जे। यथा कश्चित् अद्भुतं दृष्ट्वा विस्मयं प्राप्तः लोकहास्यमगणयित्वा विचेष्टते; तथाहमपि नानामतदर्शनादीश्वरस्य नित्यत्वानित्यत्वानामन्यतमत्वेन निर्णेतुमशक्तः सर्वप्रकारेण स्तुतिं कुर्वन् परमार्थाज्ञानित्वेन लज्जायोग्योऽपि न लज्जे इति भावः। अथ परमार्थमजानन् कथं स्तौषीत्याह—नन्विति। ननु खलु मुखरता वाचालता धृष्टा प्रगल्भा सैव बलात् मां प्रवर्तयति। अतः सैव लज्जामपहरतीति भावः॥ ९॥

ध्रुवमिति। हे पुरमथन! त्रिपुरदाहक! कश्चिद्; भाट्टमतदर्शनानुयायी सकलमिदं जगत्, ध्रुवम्; नित्यं ब्रूते। "न कदाचिदनीदृशं जगत्" इति अविनश्वरं कथयति। अपरः; अन्यः; क्षणभङ्गवादी बौद्धः, जगदिदम् अध्रुवम् क्षणिकं ब्रूते। परः; ततोऽन्यः, क्षपणकः, वीतरागी, माध्यस्थ्यमवलम्बमानः, एतस्मिन्; समस्ते; जगति, ध्रौव्याध्रौव्ये; नित्यानित्यत्वे, व्यस्तविषये; भिन्नविषये, गदति वदति। आकाशादिपञ्चकं नित्यम्। घटपटादिकमनित्यमिति ब्रूत इत्यर्थः। एवं नानाप्रकारेण वदद्भिः, तैः; वादिभिः, विस्मित इव; उपहसित इव अहं त्वां स्तुवन् जिह्रेमि; लज्जां प्राप्नोमि। अहो यद्येवं तर्हि स्तुतौ कथं प्रवर्तसे तत्राह—नन्विति। ननु अहो खलु निश्चये, मुखरता वाचालता, चपलता वा। ननु भो न धृष्टा खलु; न बलवती किम्? अपितु धृष्टैव, बलवत्येवेत्यर्थः॥ ९॥

पुरा किल ब्रह्मविष्णू अहमेव प्रधानमिति परस्परं विवादं कृतवन्तौ, तयोर्विवादभञ्जनार्थं भगवान् महेश्वरः तेजःपुञ्जतया निबध्यान्तरस्त्वेनाविर्भूतः तं दृष्ट्वा विस्मयं गतवन्तौ ब्रह्मविष्णू किमिदमिति विभाव्य निश्चयं कर्तुमूर्ध्वाधो गतवन्तौ; तन्निश्चयासमर्थौ स्वात्मनि अहंकारं मन्यमानौ तमेव प्रधानमिति मत्वा स्तुवन्तौ सन्तौ स

भगवान् स्वयमेव प्रत्यक्षतां गतः, तदैव स तेजःपुञ्जो लिङ्गरूपेणाविर्भूत इति पुराणकथामुद्भावयन् स्तौति—

तवैश्वर्यं यत्नाद् यदुपरि विरिञ्चिर्हरिरधः
परिच्छेत्तुं यातावनलमनलस्कन्दवपुषः ।
ततो भक्तिश्रद्धाभरगुरु गृणद्भ्यां गिरिश यत्
स्वयं तस्थे ताभ्यां तव किमनुवृत्तिर्न फलति ॥ १० ॥

तवेति । हे **गिरिश** ! हे शिव ! **अनलस्कन्दवपुषः**; अग्निपुञ्जशरीरस्य, **तव यत् ऐश्वर्यं** तेजोमयत्वेनाविर्भूतस्थूलरूपं, तत् **परिच्छेत्तुं** इयत्तामवधारयितुम् **उपरि** ऊर्ध्वं **विरिञ्चिः** ब्रह्मा, अधस्तात्, **हरिः** विष्णुः, **यत्नात्** सर्वयत्नेन यावद्गन्तुं शक्तौ तावदेव यातौ गतावपि अर्थात् परिच्छेत्तुं **अनलम्** असमर्थौ । **ततः** तदनन्तरं कायिकसेवारूपभक्तिमानसिकसेवारूपश्रद्धाभरेणातिशयेन **गुरु** श्रेष्ठं यथा स्यात् तथा **गृणद्भ्यां** स्तुवद्भ्यां **ताभ्यां** ब्रह्मविष्णुभ्यां **यत्** यस्मात् भगवान् स्वयमेव **तस्थे** आत्मानं प्रकाशितवान् । न तु तयोः प्रयत्नेन । अतः तव **अनुवृत्तिः** सेवा किं न फलति अपितु फलत्येव । अतः तव सेवातोऽवश्यमेव कृतकृत्यो भवतीति भावः । "स्कन्दः स्यान्नृपतावंशे संप्रदायसमूहयोः" इति मेदिनी । ताभ्याम् इति "श्लाघह्नुङ्स्थाशपां ज्ञीप्स्यमानः" इति संप्रदानम् । "भरोऽतिशयभारयोः" इति व्याडिः ॥ १० ॥

इदानीं ब्रह्मविष्णवोरनुग्रहार्थं लिङ्गोद्भवं स्तुवन्नाह—तवैश्वर्यमिति । हे गिरिश ! तव यदैश्वर्यम्; माहात्म्यम्, यत्नात्; महता प्रयत्नेन, परिच्छेत्तुम्; एतावदिति निश्चेतुम्, उपरि; ऊर्ध्वम्, विरिञ्चिः; ब्रह्मा यातः; अधः; पातालम्, हरिः; विष्णुः, यातः । द्वावपि यातौ; गतौ । अनलम्; परिच्छेत्तुमशक्तौ । कथं भूतस्य तव ? अनलस्कन्दवपुषः; अनलस्कन्दः अग्निसमूहः, वपुः शरीरं यस्य तस्य । क्वचिदनिलस्कन्दवपुष इति पाठः । तत्र वायुशरीरस्येत्यर्थः । अनलस्तम्भवपुष इति च पाठेऽप्येवमेवार्थः । ततः; पश्चात्, भक्तिश्रद्धाभरगुरुगृणद्भ्याम्; भक्तिर्भजनम्, श्रद्धा विश्वासः, तयोर्भरेण महत्वेन, गुरु; अधिकं यथा तथा, गृणद्भ्याम्; स्तुवद्भ्याम्, ताभ्याम्; ब्रह्मविष्णुभ्याम् । यद्यस्मात्कारणात् तत् तवैश्वर्यम्, स्वयं तस्थे, स्वेनैव प्रकाशितमित्यर्थः । "प्रकाशनस्थेयाख्ययोश्च"

इति तिष्ठतेरात्मनेपदम्। ताभ्यामिति तादर्थ्ये चतुर्थी। हे देव! तव अनुवृत्तिः; सेवा किं न फलति, किं न प्रयच्छति? सर्वमपि प्रयच्छतीत्यर्थः। त्वयि किमनुवृत्तिरिति पाठे, त्वयि विषये सेवा इत्यर्थः॥ १०॥

पुरा किल रावणेन नवभिर्निजशिरोभिः स्वहस्तकर्तनैः शंभोः पादपद्मोपहारं कृतमुद्भावयन् स्तौति—

अयत्नादासाद्य त्रिभुवनमवैरव्यतिकरं
दशास्यो यद्बाहूनभृत रणकण्डूपरवशान्।
शिरःपद्मश्रेणीरचितचरणाम्भोरुहबलेः
स्थिरायास्त्वद्भक्तेस्त्रिपुरहर विस्फूर्जितमिदम्॥ ११॥

अयत्नादिति। हे त्रिपुरहर! दशास्यो रावणः, न विद्यते वैरस्य विरोधस्य व्यतिकरः कारणं दर्पादिकं यत्र विरोधकारणशून्यं त्रिभुवनं स्वर्गमर्त्यपातालम्, अयत्नात् व्यापारव्यतिरेकेण आसाद्य प्राप्य रणाय युद्धाय कण्डूः खर्जूः अतिशयस्पृहा तया परवशान् तदधीनान् बाहून् विंशतिभुजान् यत् अभृत धारितवान्। इदं स्थिराया निश्चलायाः त्वयि भक्तेः विस्फूर्जितं प्रभावः। कीदृश्याः भक्तेः? शिरांस्येव पद्मश्रेणी तया रचितः कल्पितः चरणाम्भोरुहयोः पादपद्मयोः बलिः उपहारो यस्यां तथा। एतेन तत्पराक्रमं श्रुत्वा सर्वे वीरा दर्पादिकं त्यक्तवन्त इति अनायासेन विरोधकारणशून्यत्रिभुवनपतित्वमापन्नस्य रावणस्य प्रतिमल्लाभावेन युद्धनिवार्यमाणरण-कण्डूनां युद्धाभावादेव विद्यमानत्वात् तद्विशिष्टबाहुधारणं त्वयि स्थिरभक्तिसंपादि-तमिति ध्वनितम्। "कारणे च समूहे च भवेद्व्यतिकरः पुमान्" इति व्याडिः। "कण्डूः खर्जूश्च कण्डूया" इत्यमरः। "बलिः पूजोपहारः स्यात् बलिर्दानव-पुंगवः। बलिः स्त्रीमध्यभागोऽपि" इति गदसिंहः॥ ११॥

इदानीं शिवभक्त्यैकप्रवणस्य रावणस्य वृत्तान्तकथनव्याजेन तदेव द्रढयितुमाह—अयत्नादिति। हे त्रिपुरहर! दशास्यः; रावणः; अयत्नात्; अनायासेन, त्रिभुवनम्; त्रैलोक्यम्, अवैरिव्यतिकरम्; शत्रुसंपर्करहितम्, आपाद्य; संपाद्य कृत्वा, रणकण्डूपरवशान्; रणे युद्धे कण्डूः खर्जूः तया परवशान् पराधीनान्; युद्धलम्पटानित्यर्थः। बाहून्; अभृत अधत्तेति यत्, तदिदं स्थिरायाः; अचलायाः,

त्वद्भक्तेः त्वयि भक्तेः, तस्याः विस्फूर्जितम्; विस्फुरणं, विजृम्भणमिति यावत्। किं भूतायास्त्वद्भक्तेः? शिरःपद्मश्रेणीरचितचरणाम्भोरुहबलेः; शिरांस्येव पद्मानि, तेषां श्रेणी पङ्क्तिः, तया रचिता कृता, चरणाम्भोरुहयोः पादपद्मयोः, बलिः पूजोपहारः यस्यां सा तथोक्ता तस्याः। एतेन त्वयि तस्य भक्तेः फलं निरूपितम्॥ ११॥

पुरा किल भगवत्प्रसादासादितप्रचुरबाहुबलेन रावणेन एकदा मोहात् प्रतिदिनमेवं सेवार्थं कथं कैलासम् आगच्छामि कैलाससमेतं शिवं लङ्कामेव नेष्यामीति मत्वा कैलासमुत्पाटयितुमारब्धम्; ततस्तदाकर्षणकम्पितकैलासस्था पार्वती भीता शिवमालिङ्गितवती, भगवता किंचित् क्रोधेन कैलासस्थित्यर्थं अङ्गुष्ठाग्रं शनैर्व्यापारितम्, तावन्मात्रेणैव रावणो रसातलं प्राप्तः, पुनः करुणया तेनैव भगवता समुद्धृत इति पुराणोक्तरावणपराभवमुद्भावयन् स्तौति—

अमुष्य त्वत्सेवासमधिगतसारं भुजवनं
बलात्कैलासेऽपि त्वदधिवसतौ विक्रमयतः।
अलभ्या पातालेऽप्यलसचलिताङ्गुष्ठशिरसि
प्रतिष्ठा त्वय्यासीद् ध्रुवमुपचितो मुह्यति खलः॥ १२॥

अमुष्येति। हे हर! त्वत्सेवया समधिगतः प्राप्तः सारो बलं येन तादृशं **भुजवनं** बाहुसमूहं प्राप्य, **त्वदधिवसतौ** त्वदीयावासे **कैलासेऽपि विक्रमयतः बलाद्** इदमुत्पाट्य लङ्कां नेष्यामीत्यभिप्रायेण व्यापारयतः, **अमुष्य** रावणस्य **प्रतिष्ठा** स्थितिः **त्वयि** अलसं यथा स्यात् तथा चलितं प्रेरितं अङ्गुष्ठाग्रं येन तादृशि सति **पातालेऽपि** अलभ्या अप्राप्या आसीत्। अथ यत्प्रसादात् प्राप्तफलो रावणस्तमेव भगवन्तं कथं विस्मृतवानित्याह—**ध्रुवमिति**। **ध्रुवम्**; निश्चितम्, उपचितो धनादिसमृद्ध्या वृद्धिं गतः **खलः** क्रूरो जनः **मुह्यति** मूढत्वं याति। स्वोपचयकारणमपि न गणयतीत्यर्थः। चलितेति इनि दीर्घाभावः। "संज्ञापूर्वको विधिरनित्यः" इति न्यायात्॥ १२॥

इदानीं भगवति तत्कृततिरस्कारस्य फलं निरूपयति—अमुष्येति। अमुष्य; रावणस्य, पाताले; रसातलेऽपि, प्रतिष्ठा; स्थितिः, अलभ्या दुर्लभा आसीत्। किं

भूतस्य रावणस्य? भुजवनम्; बाहुसमूहम्, बलात्; शक्त्या, त्वदधिवसतौ; तव निवासस्थाने, कैलासेऽपि; विक्रमयतः; पराक्रमयतः। किं भूतं भुजवनम्? त्वत्सेवा-समधिगतसारम्; त्वत्सेवया भवदाराधनेन समधिगतः प्राप्तः सारो बलं येन तत्तथोक्तम्। कस्मिन् सति त्वयि? अलसचलिताङ्गुष्ठशिरसि सति; अलसेन अनायासेन अप्रयत्नेन चलितम् अधःकृतम् अङ्गुष्ठशिरो येन सः तथोक्तः, तस्मिन् सति। तथाहि ध्रुवम् निश्चितम् उपचितः, परया लक्ष्म्या बलेन च संपन्नः समृद्धः, खलः दुर्जनः, मुह्यति; मोहमुपगच्छति, द्रुह्यति च ॥ १२ ॥

इदानीं भगवत्सेवया बाणासुरस्य समृद्धिर्जातेति दर्शयन् स्तौति—

यदृद्धिं सुत्राम्णो वरद परमोच्चैरपि सती-
मधश्चक्रे बाणः परिजनविधेयत्रिभुवनः।
न तच्चित्रं तस्मिन् वरिवसितरि त्वच्चरणयो-
र्न कस्या उन्नत्यै भवति शिरसस्त्वय्यवनतिः ॥ १३ ॥

हे वरद! बाणः; बाणो नामासुरः, सुत्राम्णः इन्द्रस्य परमोच्चैः सतीम् अतिशयोच्चतया विद्यमानमपि ऋद्धिं संपत्तिम् अधश्चक्रे जितवान्। तत् अन्यत्र चित्रमपि त्वच्चरणयोः वरिवसितरि पूजके तस्मिन् बाणासुरे न चित्रमाश्चर्यम्। कथमित्याह—त्वयि शिरसोऽवनतिर्नमस्क्रिया कस्यै उन्नत्यै समृद्धये न भवति; अपि तु सर्वस्यै भवत्येवेति। त्वच्चरणयोर्या नमस्क्रिया मोक्षस्यापि जनयित्री तस्या इन्द्रसंपत्त्यधः-करणे कियदाश्चर्यमिति भावः। इन्द्रसंपत्त्यधःकरणमेव हेतुगर्भविशेषणमाह—बाणः कीदृशः? परिजनत्वेन विधेयं वश्यं त्रिभुवनं स्वर्गमर्त्यपातालं येन तादृशः। इन्द्रस्य केवलं स्वर्गो वश्यः, अस्य पुनस्त्रिभुवनमिति। अतोऽयमिन्द्रस्य ऋद्धिं जितवानिति भावः। वरिवस्यधातुः कण्ड्वादौ पूजायां वर्तते ॥ १३ ॥

इदानीं बाणासुरानुग्रहेण भगवन्तं स्तुवन्नाह—यदृद्धिमिति। सुत्राम्णः; वासवस्य, ऋद्धिम्; संपदम्, सुरेन्द्रत्वम् अधश्चक्रे, तिरस्कारेति यावत्। किं भूतामृद्धिम्? परमोच्चैः सतीमपि; परमोद्धताम् अतिमहतीमपीत्यर्थः। किं भूतो बाणः? परिजन-विधेयत्रिभुवनः; परिजनस्य सेवकस्य, विधेयं वश्यं, त्रिभुवनं यस्य तथोक्तः। तस्मिन्;

बाणे, तच्चित्रम्, आश्चर्यं न भवति। किं भूते बाणे? त्वच्चरणयोः वरिवसितरि; शुश्रूषके। युक्तमेतदित्याह—त्वयीति। त्वयि शिरसः; मूर्ध्नः; शिरसेति पाठान्तरम्। अवनतिः; प्रणामः, कस्या उन्नत्यै न भवति; सर्वोन्नत्यै भवत्येवेत्यर्थः॥ १३॥

इदानीं समुद्रमथनजातकालकूटविषभक्षणमुत्थापयन् स्तौति—

अकाण्डब्रह्माण्डक्षयचकितदेवासुरकृपा-
विधेयस्यासीद्यस्त्रिनयन विषं संहृतवतः।
स कल्माषः कण्ठे तव न कुरुते न श्रियमहो
विकारोऽपि श्लाघ्यो भुवनभयभङ्गव्यसनिनः॥ १४॥

अकाण्डेति। हे त्रिनयन! हे शिव! विषं गरलं संहृतवतः पीतवतः तव कण्ठे यः कल्माषः कालिमा आसीत्, स श्रियं शोभां न कुरुत इति न; अपि तु कुरुत एव। अथ भगवान् विषपानं महदनर्थहेतुं जानन्नपि कथं पीतवानित्याह—तव कीदृशस्य? अकाण्डेऽनवसरे असमये विषोर्मिवेगात् संभावितो यो ब्रह्माण्डक्षयः ब्रह्माण्डनाशः, तस्मात् चकिता भीता देवासुरा इन्द्रबलिप्रभृतयः, तेषु या कृपा दया तया विधेयस्य वश्यस्य। अन्यस्यैतद्विषपानसामर्थ्यं नास्तीति। ब्रह्मण्डप्रलयकर्तापि परकर्तृकप्रलयात् ब्रह्माण्डरक्षणाय विश्वलयकरणोद्यतं विषम् आत्मनि असाधारणप्रलयकर्तृत्वसंस्थापनाय देवासुरदयाव्याजेन स्वयमेव पीतवानिति भावः। अथात्र स कल्माषः विषप्रकारत्वेन दुष्टः स कथं भगवता धृत इत्याह—भुवनानां भयभङ्गे त्रासनाशे व्यसनिनः व्यापारयतो जनस्य विकारोऽपि श्लाघ्यः। जगदुपकारकृतं दूषणमपि भूषणमिति ध्वनितम्। "काण्डोऽस्त्री दण्डबाणार्ववर्गाव-सरवारिषु" इत्यमरः॥ १४॥

इदानीं कालकूटविषापहरणप्रतिपादनद्वारेण भगवन्तं स्तुवन्नाह—अकाण्डेति। हे त्रिनयन! विषम्; कालकूटम्; संहृतवतः; गिलितवतः, तव कण्ठे; गले, यः कल्माषः; कार्ष्ण्यम्, आसीत् संजातः। सः; कल्माषः, श्रियम्; शोभाम्, न कुरुत इति न; अपि तु कुरुत एवेत्यर्थः। तव नु कुरुत इति पाठे नुशब्दो वितर्के। श्रियं शोभां न कुरुते नु? इति। अहो; आश्चर्यम्। किं विधस्य तव? अकाण्डब्रह्माण्डक्षयचकित-

देवासुरकृपाविधेयस्य; अकाण्डे अनवसरे, अकाले, यो ब्रह्माण्डस्य क्षयः विनाशः, तस्मात् चकिताः भीताः ये देवासुराः, तेषु कृपा दया, तस्याः विधेयस्य; वश्यस्य। ननु शुद्धस्फटिकसंकाशे नीलत्वलक्षणविकारः कथं शोभां कुरुत इत्याह—विकारोऽपीति। भुवनभयभङ्गव्यसनिनः; भुवनानां भयं तस्य भङ्गे व्यसनिनः उद्युक्तस्य तव विकारोऽपि श्लाघ्यः शोभाकरः। अस्थानतः परोपकारप्रवृत्तस्य प्रकारान्तरप्राप्तविकारोऽपि श्लाघ्य इत्यर्थः॥ १४॥

इदानीं कामदेवनिग्रहमुत्थापयन् स्तौति—

असिद्धार्था नैव क्वचिदपि सदेवासुरनरे
निवर्तन्ते नित्यं जगति जयिनो यस्य विशिखाः।
स पश्यन्नीश त्वामितरसुरसाधारणमभू-
त्स्मरः स्मर्तव्यात्मा न हि वशिषु पथ्यः परिभवः॥ १५॥

असिद्धार्था इति। हे ईश! शिव! **यस्य** कामस्य **विशिखा** बाणाः **सदेवासुरनरे** देवासुरमनुष्यसहिते **जगति क्वचिदपि असिद्धार्थाः** अकृतकार्याः सन्तो न **निवर्तन्ते**; सर्वत्रैव कृतकार्या भवन्तिः; अतो **नित्यं जयिनः** सदा जयशीलाः। यस्येति विशेषणं वा। **स स्मरः** कामः **त्वाम् इतरसुरसाधारणम्**, यथा अन्ये देवास्तदधीनास्तथा त्वमपीति मत्वा अन्यदेवतुल्यं **पश्यन् स्मर्तव्यात्मा** स्मरणमात्रविषय आत्मा शरीरं यस्य तादृशो विनष्टशरीरोऽभूत्। पश्यन्निति "लक्षणहेत्वोः क्रियायाम्" इति शतृ। तेन यथा अद्वैतं पश्यन् रामं आप्नुयादिति रामप्राप्तौ अद्वैतदर्शनं हेतुः, तथा साधारणत्वेन दर्शनमेवात्मविनाशकारणमिति ध्वनितम्। अथान्यदेवतातो विशिष्टत्वमस्याजानतः कामस्य साधारणतया दर्शनं यदि शरीरनाशकं, तदा अन्येषामपि अज्ञानिनां विशिष्टतया अपश्यतां कथमेवं न कृतमित्याह—न हीति। हि यस्मात् **वशिषु** जितेन्द्रियेषु जनेषु परिभवः तिरस्कारः पथ्यो न भवति, न हितकारी भवति, केष्वपि जितेन्द्रियेषु परिभवो न पथ्यः, किंपुनः परमवशिनां वरे परमेश्वरे त्वयि चित्तविकाररूपतिरस्कारकारिणः कामस्य मङ्गलमित्यर्थः। "अनादरः परिभवः परिभावस्तिरस्क्रिया" इत्यमरः॥ १५॥

इदानीं कामनिग्रहपरं भगवन्तं स्तुवन्नाह—असिद्धार्था इति। यस्य; स्मरस्य कामस्य, जयिनः; जयशीलाः, विशिखाः; बाणाः, जगति; लोके, क्वचिदपि; कदाचिदपि, असिद्धार्थाः अकृतकार्याः न निवर्तन्ते। अपि तु कृतकार्या एव निवर्तन्त इत्यर्थः। किंभूतस्य स्मरस्य? जयिनः जयशीलस्य। किंभूते जगति? सदेवासुरनरे; देवाश्च असुराश्च नराश्च तैः सह वर्तत इति तथोक्ते; स्वर्गमर्त्यपातालेष्वपीत्यर्थः। हे ईश! सः स्मरः त्वाम् इतरसुरसाधारणम्; अन्यदेवतुल्यम्; पश्यन्; अवगच्छन्, स्मर्तव्यात्मा; स्मरणीयशरीरः अभूत; नष्टशरीरोऽभवदित्यर्थः। तथाहि वशिषु; जितेन्द्रियेषु, आत्मेश्वरेषु; परिभवः; अनादरः; अवज्ञेति यावत्। पथ्यो न हि; सुखकरो न भवतीत्यर्थः॥ १५॥

अथैकदा एको राक्षसो ब्रह्माणमाराध्य जगत् क्षयं नयामीति वरं वव्रे; ततो ब्रह्मा कालान्तरे दास्यामीति वदन् तस्थे। ततः सर्वे देवा एतद्विषयचकितमानसा हरमुपगम्य स्तुवन्तः सर्वमाचख्युः। तत्कथाश्रवणजातकुतूहलो हरो राक्षसस्य वरदाननियमितकालहरणार्थं यन्नृत्यं कृतवान् तज्जगद्रक्षणार्थमेवेति पुराणकथामुद्भावयन् स्तौति—

मही पादाघाताद्व्रजति सहसा संशयपदं
पदं विष्णोर्भ्राम्यद्भुजपरिघरुग्णग्रहगणम्।
मुहुर्द्यौर्दौस्थ्यं यात्यनिभृतजटाताडिततटा
जगद्रक्षायै त्वं नटसि ननु वामैव विभुता॥ १६॥

महीति। हे ईश! त्वं जगद्रक्षायै नटसि नृत्यसि। जगन्ति पुनस्तव ताण्डवनटनाघातयोगात् संशयापन्नानीति प्रकाशयति। नृत्यतस्तव पादाघातात् पादाघातं प्राप्य मही पृथिवी सहसा तत्क्षणमेव प्रलयकाल इति संशयपदं संशयस्थानं व्रजति प्राप्नोति। तथा विष्णोः पदम्, आकाशं भ्राम्यत् चन्द्रसूर्यभ्रमणेन भ्रमदिव। कीदृशम्? तव भुजा एव परिघा अतिसुवृत्तपीवरदृढदीर्घास्तैः रुग्णा पीडिता ग्रहगणाः सूर्यादयो यत्र तादृशम्। यद्वा—भ्राम्यद्भिः भुजपरिघैः रुग्णा ग्रहगणा यत्र तादृशमाकाशं संशयं गच्छतीति पूर्वेणान्वयः। यद्यपि "वियद्विष्णुपदम्" इति कोशे संहितक्रमोक्तविष्णुपदोऽयं शब्द आकाशवचनः, तथापि भूरिप्रयोगदर्शनात्

विगृहीतक्रमोक्तोऽपि आकाशपर्याय इति भट्टिटीकायां व्याख्यातमिति। तथा द्यौः स्वर्गः अनिभृता या जटास्ताभिस्ताडितस्तटः प्रान्तभागो यस्याः तादृशी सती दौस्थ्यं मुहुर्दुस्थतां याति। ननु सर्वज्ञो भगवान् जगदपायमगणयन् किमित्येवं नृत्यति, अत आह—नन्विति। अहो विभुता प्रभुता वामैव प्रतिकूलैव जगतोऽनुकूलाचरणे किंचित् प्रतिकूलता भवत्येव 'राजराक्षसन्यायात्'। यथा राक्षसेन भोक्तुमारब्धस्य राज्यस्य रक्षणार्थं राक्षसवधाय गच्छतो राज्ञः सहचरसेनाभिर्ग्रामस्य कस्यचित् पीडनात् प्रतिकूलतेति ॥ १६ ॥

अधिकबलवान् कश्चन राक्षसः संध्यासमये जगदिदं क्षयितुमुद्यतः। तन्निवारणाय तस्मिन् काले भगवान् ताण्डवं करोति स्म। संप्रति तस्येश्वरस्य ताण्डवसंबन्धां स्तुतिमाह—महीति। हे देव! जगद्रक्षायै; लोकपालनाय, त्वम्; नटसि नृत्यसि, ताण्डवं करोषि। भो स्वामिन्! तव विभुता; महत्वं, वामैव विपरीतैव। कथमित्याह—मही; पृथिवी, पादाघातात्; पादताडनात, सहसा; शीघ्रम्, संशयपदं व्रजति। अस्तिनास्तीति संदेहं गच्छतीत्यर्थः। तथा विष्णोः पदम्; आकाशः, भ्राम्यद्भुजपरिघरुग्णग्रहगणम्; भ्राम्यन्त इतस्ततश्चलन्तस्ते च ते भुजाश्च, त एव परिघा अर्गलाः, तै रुग्णः भग्नः, ग्रहाणां नक्षत्राणां गणः समूहो यस्मिन् तत्तथोक्तम्। अन्यच्च वैपरीत्यम्; द्यौः; स्वर्गः, मुहुर्मुहुः, दौस्थ्यम्; दुस्थत्वं याति। सा किं विधा? अनिभृतजटाताडिततटा; अनिभृताभिः अनिश्चलाभिः जटाभिः ताडितं तटं पार्श्वं यस्याः सा तथोक्ता ॥ १६ ॥

इदानीं गङ्गाधरणेन भगवच्छरीरमहत्त्वं प्रकटयन् स्तौति—

वियद्व्यापी तारागणगुणितफेनोद्गमरुचिः
प्रवाहो वारां यः पृषतलघुदृष्टः शिरसि ते।
जगद्द्वीपाकारं जलधिवलयं तेन कृतमि-
त्यनेनैवोन्नेयं धृतमहिम दिव्यं तव वपुः ॥ १७ ॥

वियदिति। हे ईश! यो वारां प्रवाहः गङ्गाजलप्रवाहः स वियद्व्यापी मन्दाकिनीसंज्ञया आकाशव्यापकः। कीदृशः? तारागणेन नक्षत्रवृन्देन स्वान्तःपातिना गुणिता शुभ्रत्वादिगुणसजातीयत्वात् वर्धिता फेनोद्गमरुचिर्यस्य तादृशः। यद्वा तारागणेन गुणितः संख्यातो यः फेनस्तस्योद्गमेन रुचिर्यस्य असंख्यफेनोद्गमरुचिरित्यर्थः। यद्वा तारागणानां

यो गुणः श्वेतत्वं तद्विशिष्टानां फेनानाम् उद्गमेन रुचिर्यस्य। गुणशब्दादस्त्यर्थे इतच्। सोऽयं वारां प्रवाहः ते तव शिरसि पृषतलघुदृष्टः पृषतात् बिन्दोरपि लघु अल्पं यथा स्यात् तथा जनैर्दृष्ट उपलब्धः। तेन पश्चात् पृथिव्यामागतेन प्रवाहेण जगत् महीमण्डलं जलधिवलयं द्वीपाकारं च कृतम्। अगस्त्येन समुद्रेषु पीतेषु पुनर्भगीरथानीतगङ्गाजलेन तेषां पूरणात् समुद्राणां जलधित्वेन जलधिरेव वलयः वेष्टनं यस्य तादृशं कृतम्। तथा तज्जलपूरितसमुद्रैरखण्डमहीतलस्य सप्तधा खण्डितत्वात् जम्बूद्वीपादि सप्त आकारा रूपाणि यस्य तादृशं कृतमिति। अनेनैव प्रकारेण तव वपुः शरीरं दिव्यम् अलौकिकं धृतमहिम च। सर्वेभ्यो महत्तरम् अतिबृहच्च उन्नेयम् ज्ञातव्यमित्यर्थः। यस्य शिरसि आकाशव्यापकसमुद्रपूरकजलप्रवाहो बिन्दुतोऽपि अल्पदृष्टः स्यात्, तस्य तव शरीरेयत्ता अनवधारणीया इत्यनुमीयत इति भावः। "पृषन्ति बिन्दुपृषताः" इत्यमरः। अत्र जगच्छब्दो महीमण्डलमात्रोपलक्षणः, द्वीपादिविशेषणात् ॥ १७ ॥

पूर्वमगस्त्यमुनिना हस्तपात्रीकृतो जलधिः, तेन पुनः पीतः सर्वदेवाभ्यर्थितेन भगवता गङ्गाजलैः पूरित इत्येतत्संबन्धां स्तुतिमाह—वियदिति। हे देव! वाराम्; गङ्गापयसां, यः प्रवाहः ओघः वियद्व्यापी सः प्रवाहः तव शिरसि जटाजूटमकुटे पृषतवत् जलबिन्दुवत् लघु सूक्ष्मं यथा तथा दृष्टः। वियदाकाशं व्याप्तुं शीलमस्य तथोक्तः। पुनः किं विधः? तारागणगुणितफेनोद्गमरुचिः; ताराणां नक्षत्राणां गणः समूहः तेन गुणिताः फेनोद्गमस्य डिण्डीरोत्पत्तेः रुचिः शोभा यस्य सः। फेनप्रवाहेण जगत् द्वीपाकारं कृतम्, जलमध्ये स्थितो भूखण्डो द्वीपः, तद्रूपमकारि। किं विधम् जगत्? जलधिवलयम्; जलधिः समुद्रः वलयः परिधिः यस्य तत्तथोक्तम्। तेनैव हेतुना तव दिव्यं सदानन्दात्मकं वपुः शरीरं धृतमहिमेत्युन्नेयम्। धृतो महिमा सर्वज्ञत्वं सर्वदर्शित्वं सर्वकर्तृत्वं च येन वपुषा तत्तथोक्तमित्युन्नेयम् ॥ १७ ॥

इदानीं त्रिपुरदाहमुद्भावयन् स्तौति—

रथः क्षोणी यन्ता शतधृतिरगेन्द्रो धनुरथो
रथाङ्गे चन्द्रार्कौ रथचरणपाणिः शर इति।
दिधक्षोस्ते कोऽयं त्रिपुरतृणमाडम्बरविधि-
र्विधेयैः क्रीडन्त्यो न खलु परतन्त्राः प्रभुधियः ॥ १८ ॥

रथ इति। हे ईश! **त्रिपुरतृणं दिधक्षोः** दग्धुमिच्छोस्तव **कोऽयमाडम्बरविधिः** परिपाटी। महत्प्रयोजनमुद्दिश्यैव महत्परिपाटी क्रियते; न हि नखच्छेद्ये वस्तुनि लोकाः कुठारं परिगृह्णन्ति। अतस्त्वदनायासनाश्यत्रिपुरदाहे एतादृशी परिपाटी नोचितेति कोऽयमित्युक्तम्। अनायासनाश्यत्वात् त्रिपुरे तृणरूपकमित्यर्थः। परिपाटीमेवाह—त्रिपुरदाहे **क्षोणी** पृथिवी तव **रथः** स्यन्दन आसीत्। एवं **शतधृतिः** इन्द्रो यन्ता सारथिरासीत्। **अगेन्द्रः** पर्वतप्रधानः मेरुः **धनुः** आसीत्। **अथोशब्दः** अथशब्दवदव्ययः वाक्यभेदार्थः। **चन्द्रार्कौ** चन्द्रसूर्यौ **रथाङ्गे** चक्रे आस्ताम्। **रथचरणपाणिः**; रथचरणं चक्रं पाणौ हस्ते यस्य तादृशो विष्णुः **शरः** बाण आसीत्। इतिशब्दः एवंप्रकारार्थः। इच्छामात्रेण त्रिभुवनं संहृतवतस्तव एवंप्रकारेणरण सामग्रीरचनेन किं प्रयोजनमिति भावः। एवमाक्षिप्य परिहरति—**विधेयैरिति।** खलु निश्चितं **प्रभुधियः** प्रभोरीश्वरस्य बुद्धयः **परतन्त्राः** पराधीना न भवन्ति; किं तु स्वतन्त्रा एव। कीदृश्यः? **विधेयैः** आज्ञावशैर्द्रव्यैः क्रीडन्त्यः, न हि क्रीडायां प्रयोजनाद्यपेक्षास्ति। अनायासेन सर्वं कर्तुं क्षमस्य तव लोकवदीहमानबुद्धेः न किंचिदप्यनुचितमिति भावः। "आडम्बरस्तूर्यरवे परिपाट्यां गजस्वने" इति **शाब्दिकनरसिंहः**। "परतन्त्रः पराधीनः परवान् नाथवानपि" इत्यमरः। "पुरुहूतः शतधृतिर्जिष्णुर्देवपतिस्तथा" इति **मञ्जरी** ॥ १८ ॥

संप्रतीश्वरस्य त्रिपुरदहनाडम्बरविषयां स्तुतिमाह—**रथ इति।** हे देव! त्रिपुराण्येव तृणं दिधक्षोः दग्धुमिच्छोः ते तव कोऽयमाडम्बरविधिः कोऽयं संभ्रमः? अयं संभ्रमः किमर्थमिति यावत्। तमेवाडम्बरं दर्शयन्नाह—रथः इति। रथः क्षोणी; भूमिः। यन्ता सारथिः, शतधृतिः ब्रह्मा। अगेन्द्रः; मेरुः, धनुः चापः। अथो; अनन्तरम्। रथाङ्गे रथचक्रे, चन्द्रार्कौ; सोमसूर्यौ। रथचरणपाणिः; चक्रपाणिः विष्णुः, शरः; बाणः। इतिशब्दः प्रकारवचने। अथवा युक्तमेवैतत्। प्रभुधियः स्वामिनां बुद्धयः फलतन्त्रा न खलु; फलप्रधाना न भवन्ति। यावता फलं सिध्यति, तावदेव न संपादयन्तीत्यर्थः। किं विधाः प्रभुधियः? विधेयैः; भृत्यजनैः सह क्रीडन्त्यः विनोदयन्त्यः ॥ १८ ॥

इदानीं विष्णोरतिशयभक्तिदर्शनात् चक्रदानमाह—

हरिस्ते साहस्रं कमलबलिमाधाय पदयो-
र्यदेकोने तस्मिन् निजमुदहरन्नेत्रकमलम् ।
गतो भक्त्युद्रेकः परिणतिमसौ चक्रवपुषा
त्रयाणां रक्षायै त्रिपुरहर जागर्ति जगताम् ॥ १९ ॥

हरिरिति । हे **त्रिपुरहर!** हे शिव ! **हरिः** विष्णुः **ते** तव **पदयोः** चरणयोः **साहस्रं** सहस्रसंख्याकं **कमलबलिं** पद्मपूजोपहारं सहस्रसंख्याकपूजोपहारं पद्ममिति यावत् । **आधाय** एकत्रीकृत्य, अथ **तस्मिन्** कमले **एकोने** एकहीने सति **यत् निजं** स्वकीयं **नेत्रकमलं** नयनपद्मम् **उदहरत्** सहस्रपूरणार्थं निजचक्षुःपद्ममुत्पाटितवान् । **असौ भक्त्युद्रेकः** भक्तेरतिशयत्वं स्वयमेव **चक्रवपुषा** चक्रशरीरेण **परिणतिं** निष्पत्तिं **गतः** सन् **त्रयाणां जगतां रक्षायै** स्वर्गमर्त्यपातालानां रक्षायै **जागर्ति** प्रवर्तते । अत्रेयं पुराणकथा—पुरा किल विष्णुः सहस्रपद्मेन प्रत्यहं शिवं पूजितवान् । तत्रैकस्मिन् दिने विष्णोर्भक्तिं जिज्ञासुना हरेण एकत्रीकृतसहस्रकमलात् एकं कमलं हृतम् । ततः सहस्रकमलदानसमये तत्रैकोनं ज्ञात्वा तदानीमन्यदप्राप्यं बुद्ध्वा नियमभङ्गभयेन भक्त्यतिशयत्वाच्च निजचक्षुःपद्ममुत्पाट्य कमलानां सहस्रं पूरयित्वा शिवचरणयोर्ददौ । अनया भक्त्या तुष्टः शिवः जगद्रक्षाकरणयोग्यसुदर्शननामचक्रं विष्णवे ददौ । तेनैव चक्रेण विष्णुर्जगद्रक्षतीति भक्तिरेव मूर्त्तिमच्चक्रं भूतेति ॥ १९ ॥

पूर्वं महादेवः हरेः चक्रं दत्तवानिति तत्संबन्धां स्तुतिमाह—हरिरिति । हे त्रिपुरहर ! हरिः; नारायणः, ते; तव, पदयोः; चरणयोः, साहस्रम्, सहस्रसंख्यापरिमितम्, कमलबलिम्; कमलानां बलिम् पद्मपूजाम् आधाय; निक्षिप्य, तस्मिन्; बलौ, एकोने; एकेन कमलेन ऊने हीने सति । निजम्; आत्मीयम्, नेत्रकमलम्; उदहरत् उद्धृतवान् इति यत् असौ भक्त्युद्रेकः; भक्त्यतिशयः, चक्रवपुषा; चक्ररूपेण परिणतिम्; परिणामम्, गतः; प्राप्तः सन्, त्रयाणां जगताम्; स्वर्गमर्त्यपातालानाम्, रक्षायै; त्राणायैव जागर्ति प्रबुध्यति अप्रमत्तस्तिष्ठतीत्यर्थः ॥ १९ ॥

संप्रति भगवतो यज्ञफलदानकर्तृत्वमुद्भावयन् स्तौति—

क्रतौ सुप्ते जाग्रत्त्वमसि फलयोगे क्रतुमतां
क्व कर्म प्रध्वस्तं फलति पुरुषाराधनमृते ।
अतस्त्वां संप्रेक्ष्य क्रतुषु फलदानप्रतिभुवं
श्रुतौ श्रद्धां बद्ध्वा दृढपरिकरः कर्मसु जनः ॥ २० ॥

क्रताविति। **क्रतौ** यज्ञे **सुप्ते** विनष्टे सति **क्रतुमतां** याज्ञिकानां जनानां **फलयोगे** यज्ञफलेन सह यज्ञकारिसंयोगे त्वं जाग्रदसि त्वं यज्ञफलदायको भवसि । यतः **पुरुषाराधनमृते** परमपुरुषस्य ईश्वरस्य भवत आराधनं विना **प्रध्वस्तं** कर्म यज्ञादि **क्व**? कस्मिन् काले देशे पुरुषे वा **फलति** फलदं भवति ; अपितु नैव । तस्मात्त्वाराधनमेव यज्ञफलकारणमिति भावः । **अतः** कारणात् यज्ञकारी जनः **त्वां क्रतुषु** यज्ञेषु **फलदानप्रतिभुवं** फलदानकर्तारं **संप्रेक्ष्य** ज्ञात्वा **श्रुतौ** वेदवाक्ये श्रद्धाम् आदरं **बद्ध्वा** कृत्वा **कर्मसु** यज्ञेषु **दृढपरिकरः** दृढारम्भो भवति । अयंभावः—यागस्तु क्रिया सा च उत्पत्तिविनाशधर्मयोगादनित्या, फलं च कालान्तरे लोकान्तरे च लभ्यम्, ततश्च विनष्टे यागे यागफलं कथं लभ्यते? इत्याशङ्कायां यज्ञकर्मानुष्ठाने परमपुरुषाराधनमेव यागफलदमिति निश्चित्य "स्वर्गकामोऽश्वमेधेन यजेत" इत्यादियागप्रवर्त्तकवेदवाक्ये आदरं कृत्वा याज्ञिको लोकान्तरफलमपि कर्म आरभते इति यज्ञफलदाने भवानेव कर्तेति संक्षेपः । "आरम्भे च समूहे च भवेत् परिकरः पुमान्" इति व्याडिः । "प्रतिभूर्नायकः कर्ता क्रियानुष्ठानदर्शकः" इति शाब्दिकनरसिंहः ॥ २० ॥

इदानीं मीमांसावादी वेदस्य नित्यतां मन्यमानः, "न कदाचिदनीदृशं जगत्" इति प्रतिपद्यते । भगवतो जगत्कर्तृत्वं प्रतिपाद्य तन्मतनिराकरणद्वारेणैवं स्तोतुमाह—क्रताविति । हे देव! यागस्य क्रियात्मकत्वेनोत्पत्तिप्रध्वंसित्वं नष्टत्वं चास्ति । क्रतौ सुप्ते विनिष्टे, क्रतुमताम्; यज्वनां, फलयोगे; स्वर्गादिफलसंबन्धे, त्वम्; जाग्रद् असि; फलं दातुं सावधानोऽसि । कथमेतत्? प्रध्वस्तम्; विनष्टं कर्म क्रिया, पुरुषाराधनमृते; ईश्वराराधनं विना, क्व फलति; न कुत्रापि फलतीत्यर्थः । अतः कारणात् जनः; लोकः, क्रतुषु फलदानप्रतिभुवम्; फलदातारम् त्वाम् संप्रेक्ष्य विचार्य, श्रुतौ; वेदवाक्ये, श्रद्धां बद्ध्वा विश्वासं कृत्वा, कर्मसु; योगेषु, दृढपरिकरः; कृतप्रयत्न इति ॥ २० ॥

इदानीं परमपुरुषमहादेवाराधनव्यतिरेकेण समस्तोपकरणान्वितोऽपि यागो नष्ट इति प्रदर्शयन् स्तौति—

क्रियादक्षो दक्षः क्रतुपतिरधीशस्तनुभृता-
मृषीणामार्त्विज्यं शरणद सदस्याः सुरगणाः।
क्रतुभ्रंशस्त्वत्तः क्रतुफलविधानव्यसनिनो
ध्रुवं कर्तुः श्रद्धाविधुरमभिचाराय हि मखाः ॥ २१ ॥

क्रियेति। हे शरणद! हे महादेव, यत्र क्रतौ दक्षः प्रजापतिः, क्रतुपतिः यज्ञाधिकारी सोऽपि क्रियादक्षः क्रियासु दक्षः यज्ञक्रियाकुशलः; तथा तनुभृतां शरीरिणाम् अधीशः राजा, तथा यत्र ऋषीणाम्, वसिष्ठादीनाम् आर्त्विज्यम्; ऋत्विक्कर्म, तथा यत्र सुरगणाः ब्रह्मादयः, सदस्याः विधिदर्शिनः, एवंभूतस्यापि क्रतोः यज्ञस्य क्रतुफलविधानव्यसनिनः यज्ञफलविधानरसिकात् त्वत्तः भवत्—सकाशात् भ्रंशः नाश इति। कथमित्याह—हि यस्मात् श्रद्धाविधुरं श्रद्धाविहीनं यथा स्यात् तथा क्रियमाणा मखा यज्ञाः कर्तुः यज्ञकारिणः, अभिचाराय हिंसार्थं भवन्तीति ध्रुवं निश्चितमित्यर्थः। यत एवं साधनसंपन्नोऽपि यागस्तवाराधनविरहात् त्वत्तो नष्टः, तत एव यज्ञफलं तवाराधनकारणमिति भावः। दक्षे हि त्वामनादृत्यान्यदेवानाहूय यज्ञे प्रवृत्ते निजकन्यया सत्या पत्यवमानमसहमानया शरीरत्यागेन जनितक्रोधेन शिवेन यज्ञो ध्वस्त इति कालिकापुराणसंवादः "हीने कुण्डे च वैकल्ये विधुरं वाच्यवद्भवेत्" इति चन्द्रः ॥ २१ ॥

इममेवार्थं दक्षयागभ्रंशदृष्टान्तेन दृढीकुर्वन्नाह—क्रियेति। हे शरणद! क्रियासु; यागक्रियासु दक्षः, कुशलः; दक्षः; दक्षप्रजापतिः, क्रतुपतिः; यजमानः। स किंभूतः? तनुभृताम्; शरीरिणाम्, अधीशः; अधिपतिः, प्रजापतित्वात्। ऋषीणामार्त्विज्यम्; ऋषयो वसिष्ठादयः एव ऋत्विज इत्यर्थः; सुरगणाः; इन्द्रादय एव, सदस्याः; सदसि स्थिताः। एवंविधसामग्रीकस्यापि दक्षस्य, त्वत्तः; भवतः सकाशादेव, क्रतुभ्रेषः; यागक्रियाभ्रंशः, अभूदित्यर्थः। क्रतुभ्रंश इति पाठेऽप्येवमेवार्थः। किंविधाद्भवतः? क्रतुफलदानव्यसनिनः; क्रतुषु यागेषु फलस्य दाने उत्सुकात्। एतदुक्तं भवति—त्वयि भक्तिहीनत्वात् दक्षस्येप्सितफलप्राप्तिर्न संजातेति युक्तमेवैतत्। ध्रुवम्; निश्चितम्।

श्रद्धाविधुरम्; विश्वासरहितं यथा तथा, कर्तुः; कुर्वतः पुरुषस्य, मखाः, यागाः अभिचाराय अनर्थाय भवन्ति हि ॥ २१ ॥

पुरा किल ब्रह्मा निजदुहितरं संध्यामतिसुन्दरीं वीक्ष्य कामुकोऽतिकान्तुमुपचक्रमे। हरिणी भूत्वा धावन्तीं तामपि संध्यां हरिणशरीरधारिणो ब्रह्मणो रन्तुमनुधावतोऽयोग्यजिहीर्षया तस्मिन् मृगरूपे ब्रह्मणि धनुष्पाणिः शिवः व्याधरूपेणानुगतः सन् बाणं क्षिप्तवान्। सोऽपि मृगः पलायमान आकाशं गतोऽपि तेन बाणेन भिन्न आकाशे तारागणरूपेण दृश्यत इति मार्कण्डेयपुराणसंवादेन स्तौति—

प्रजानाथं नाथ प्रसभमभिकं स्वां दुहितरं
गतं रोहिद्भूतां रिरमयिषुमृष्यस्य वपुषा।
धनुष्पाणेर्यातं दिवमपि सपत्राकृतममुं
त्रसन्तं तेऽद्यापि त्यजति न मृगव्याधरभसः ॥ २२ ॥

प्रजेति। हे नाथ! हे हर, धनुष्पाणेः धनुर्हस्तस्य तव मृगव्याधरभसः मृगे व्याधस्येव उद्यमः ताडनानुरागो वा, अद्यापि एवंभूतं प्रजानाथं ब्रह्माणं न त्यजति। अद्यापि मृगरूपे ब्रह्मणि व्याधरूपस्य तव बाणव्यापार आस्त इत्यर्थः। प्रजानाथं कीदृशम्? अभिकं कामुकम्। पुनः कीदृशम्? ऋश्यस्य वपुषा मृगशरीरेण रोहिद्भूतां मृगीभूतां स्वां दुहितरं निजकन्यां प्रसभं बलात्कारेण रिरमयिषुं रन्तुमिच्छुम्। पुनः कीदृशम्? त्रसन्तं भीतम् अतो दिवमपि यातं तथापि सपत्राकृतं बाणव्यथितम्। "सपत्रनिष्पत्रादतिव्यथने" इति लमादित्वात् डाचि निपातः। "कामुकोऽभिकः" इत्यमरः। 'गोकर्णपृषतैणर्श्यरोहिताश्चमरो मृगाः" इत्यमरः। "उद्यमे चानुरागे च निर्जने रभसः पुमान्" इति व्याडिः ॥ २२ ॥

संप्रति ब्रह्मणो दुहित्रभिलाषुकस्य निग्रहसामर्थ्यमैश्वर्यं स्तुवन्नाह—प्रजानाथमिति। नाथेत्यादिना आखेटवृत्तिं दर्शयति। हे नाथ! स्वामिन्, धनुः पाणौ यस्य धनुष्पाणेः, "प्रहरणार्थेभ्यः परे निष्ठा सप्तम्यौ" इति सप्तम्यन्तस्य परनिपातः। ते तव मृगव्याधरभसः; मृगयावेगः, अमुम् प्रजानाथम्; ब्रह्माणम्, अद्यापि न त्यजति न मुञ्चति। किं

भूतं प्रजानाथम्? अभिकम्; कामुकम्। अत एव स्वां दुहितरम्; स्वसुताम्। ऋश्यस्य वपुषा; मृगशरीरेण, प्रसभम्; बलात्कारेण, रिरमयिषुम्; रन्तुमिच्छन्तम्। किं विधां दुहितरम्? रोहिद्भूताम् मृगरूपाम्; मृगीजातामित्यर्थः। पुनः किं विधं प्रजानाथम्? त्रसन्तम्; भीतम्। अत एव दिवम् अपि; आकाशमपि। यातम्; गतम्। पुनः किंविधम्? सपत्राकृतम्; बाणेन विद्धं सपत्रं शरमस्य शरीरे प्रवेशितमित्यर्थः। ब्रह्मा कामुकत्वेन मृगीभूतां स्वसुतां मृगरूपेण रन्तुं गतः। अधर्मिणमेनं ब्रह्माणं शरेण हन्तुमीश्वरो मृगयुर्भूत्वा तौ द्वावप्यनुयातीत्यार्थः। इदानीमपि तौ गगने तथा दृश्येते ॥ २२ ॥

इदानीं भगवतः शरीरेण पत्नीशरीरघटनायां सत्यामपि स्त्रीवशतां निरस्यन् स्तौति—

स्वलावण्याशंसा धृतधनुषमह्नाय तृणवत्
पुरः प्लुष्टं दृष्ट्वा पुरमथन पुष्पायुधमपि।
यदि स्त्रैणं देवी यमनियतदेहार्धघटना-
दवैति त्वामद्धा बत वरद मुग्धा युवतयः ॥ २३ ॥

स्वलावण्येति। हे पुरमथन! हे वरद! देवी; पार्वती, स्वलावण्याशंसा; स्वकीयसौन्दर्यप्रशंसाकारिणी सती, धृतधनुषम्; धनुर्धरम्, पुष्पायुधम्; कामदेवं, पुरः; साक्षात् त्वया तृणवत् प्लुष्टं दृष्टिपातेनैव दग्धम्। दृष्ट्वापि यदि यमनियतदेहार्धघटनात्; संयमासादितशरीरार्धदानरूपचेष्टातः, त्वां स्त्रैणं; स्त्रीवशमवैति जानाति। बतेति खेदे। सर्वा युवतयः स्त्रियो मुग्धा अज्ञाः, अद्धा निश्चितमेव। निश्चये अद्धेत्यव्ययम्। मम सौन्दर्यं दृष्ट्वा भगवान् मां देहार्धे धृतवान्। अथवा मम लावण्यवशीभूतो भगवान् निजदेहार्धं मह्यं दत्तवानिति गर्वं यदि कामदमनं दृष्ट्वापि करोति भ्रान्तचित्तत्वात् साधारणस्त्रीस्वभावं गतवती पार्वती कथमन्यस्त्रीजनतः अधिका भवेदिति सर्वा युवतयो मुग्धा इत्युक्तम्। न हि मन्मथघाती पुरुषः क्वापि स्त्रीवशः स्यात्, स्त्रैणतां प्रति मन्मथाच्छन्नत्वेन कारणत्वात्। अह्नाय झटिति दग्धं दृष्ट्वा इत्यन्वयः। "स्राग्झटित्यञ्जसाह्नाय" इत्यव्ययेऽमरः। स्त्रैणमिति "स्त्रीपुंभ्यां नञ्स्नञौ भवनात्" इत्यादिना स्त्रियो णन् प्रत्ययः। "स्यात् पुरः पुरतोऽग्रतः" इत्यव्ययेऽमरः।

"तत्त्वे त्वद्धाञ्जसा द्वयम्" इत्यव्ययेऽमरः। तत्त्वं निश्चितं यमेन संयमेन नियतो वशीकृतो यो देहस्तदर्धे देव्याः शरीरार्धस्य घटनात् योजनात्। यमनियतेत्यनेन तस्याभिलाषुकत्वाशङ्का निराकृतेति व्याख्यान्तरम् ॥ २३ ॥

इदानीं गौरीरूपाभिमानप्रकटनपुरःसरं भगवतः परमयोगित्वं स्तोतुमाह—स्वलावण्येति। हे पुरमथन! हे त्रिपुरदहन! अह्नाय; शीघ्रम्, तृणवत्; तृणमिव, प्लुष्टम्; दग्धम्, धृतधनुषम्; गृहीतचापम्, पुष्पायुधम्; मन्मथम्, पुरः; अग्रतः, दृष्ट्वापि, देवी; गौरी, यमनियतदेहार्धघटनात्; यमनियतदेहो यमप्राप्तदेहः, तस्यार्धे घटनात् योजनात्, "अर्धं नपुंसकम्" इति समासः। यमनिरत देहार्धघटनादिति पाठे, हे यमनिरत! यमाद्यष्टाङ्गयोगसंसक्त, देहार्धघटनात् शरीरार्धयोजनादिति। त्वाम् स्त्रैणम्; स्त्रीपरतन्त्रम्, अवैति, यदि जानाति चेत्, तर्हि हे वरद! अद्धा; निश्चितम्, युवतयः; स्त्रियः मुग्धाः; अज्ञाः, बत अहो। किं भूता गौरी? स्वलावण्याशंसा; आत्मसौन्दर्यं कीर्तयन्ती; स्वकीयरूपाभिमानिनीत्यर्थः ॥ २३ ॥

अन्यपुरुषो यद्यमङ्गलशीलो भवति, तदा स निन्द्यः, भगवांस्तु सदा अमङ्गलशीलोऽपि स्मर्तॄणां परममङ्गलद एवेति पुरुषान्तरादाधिक्यमुद्भावयन् अपूर्वपुरुषतामाह—

श्मशानेष्वाक्रीडाः स्मरहर पिशाचाः सहचरा-
श्चिताभस्मालेपः स्रगपि नृकरोटीपरिकरः।
अमङ्गल्यं शीलं तव भवतु नामैवमखिलं
तथापि स्मर्तॄणां वरद परमं मङ्गलमसि ॥ २४ ॥

श्मशानेष्विति। हे स्मरहर! कामनाशक! हे वरद! यद्यपि तव एवंभूतम् अमङ्गल्यं अकल्याणकारणं शीलं स्वभावो भवतु; तथापि तव अखिलं नाम समस्तनामधेयम्, उग्रः, कपालभृत्, श्मशानवासीत्यादिरूपं स्मर्तॄणां स्मरणकारिणां त्वं परमं मङ्गलम् उत्तमकल्याणकरोऽसि। अमङ्गल्यमेवाह—श्मशानेष्विति। श्मशानेषु; मृतदाहस्थानेषु, आक्रीडा; भ्रमणखेलनादिक्रीडनम्। पिशाचाः; प्रेताः, सहचराः; अनुचराः। चिताभस्मभिरालेपः; शरीरलेपनम्। नृकरोटीपरिकरः; मनुष्यशिरोस्थिसमूहः, स्रक्; माला यस्य, एतादृशव्यापारस्तस्य शीलं अमङ्गल्यमेवेति। ईश्वरस्य

एतादृशव्यापारे सत्यपि तत्तद्व्यापारजन्यदोषभाक्त्वं नास्त्येव। महापुरुषत्वादिति सर्वोत्कृष्टत्वं प्रतिपादितमिति भावः। "शिरोस्थनि करोटिः स्त्री" इत्यमरः। "शीलं स्वभावे सद्वृत्ते" इत्यमरः। "आरम्भे च समूहे च भवेत् परिकरः पुमान्" इति व्याडिः। अखिलं नाम स्मर्तॄणामिति स्मरणार्थयोगे कर्मणि न षष्ठी, उत्तरत्र नित्यग्रहणेनानित्यत्वकल्पनादिति तत्रैवोक्तम् ॥ २४ ॥

संप्रति स्वेच्छानर्तनपुरःसरं भगवतः परममङ्गलप्रदत्वं स्तुवन्नाह—श्मशानेष्विति। हे स्मरहर! तव श्मशानेषु; पितृवनेषु, आक्रीडा; आ समन्तात् क्रीडा, विहरणमिति यावत्। तथा पिशाचाः; वेतालादयः, सहचराः; सहवासिनः। तथा आलेपः; अनुलेपनम्, चिताभस्म; मृतशरीरदहनार्थोपचितकाष्ठनिचयः, चिता, तन्मयं भसितं भस्म। तव स्रगपि; मालापि, नृकरोटीपरिकरः; नरकपालसमूहः। एवम्; अनेन प्रकारेण, तव अखिलम् समग्रम्; शीलं स्वभावः, अमङ्गल्यम्; अशुभं भवतु नाम; तथापि स्मर्तॄणाम्; चिन्तयतां भक्तानाम्; हे वरद! त्वाम्, परमम्; उत्कृष्टं मङ्गलप्रदोऽसि ॥ २४ ॥

संप्रति परमब्रह्मत्वेन संस्थापयन् स्तौति—

मनः प्रत्यक्चित्ते सविधमवधायात्तमरुतः

प्रहृष्यद्रोमाणः प्रमदसलिलोत्सङ्गितदृशः।

यदालोक्याह्लादं ह्रद इव निमज्ज्यामृतमये

दधत्यन्तस्तत्त्वं किमपि यमिनस्तत् किल भवान् ॥ २५ ॥

मन इत्यादि। प्रत्यक्चित्ते; प्रति अञ्चतीति क्विप् प्रत्यक्, प्रतिगतं चित्तं येन स परमात्मा तस्मिन् परमात्मनि। यमिनः; योगिनो जनाः। सविधं सम्यक् यथा स्यात् तथा मन अवधाय निवेश्य, यत् किमपि अनिर्वचनीयम्, अन्तस्तत्त्वं ब्रह्मस्वरूपम् आलोक्य आह्लादं परमसुखं दधति धारयन्ति। तदन्तस्तत्त्वं भवानेव, किलेति निश्चये। अमृतमये ह्रदे; अमृतपरिपूर्णे सरसि, निमज्ज्य इव; यथा अमृतसरोवरमग्ना जना आह्लादं सुखं गच्छन्ति, तथा योगिनोऽपि ब्रह्मदर्शनादाह्लादं दधति धारन्तीति भावः। योगिनः कीदृशाः? आत्तमरुतः; आत्ताः पूरककुम्भकरेचकैः प्राणायामैर्वशीकृता मरुतो देहचारिवायवो यैः। पुनः कीदृशाः?

प्रहृष्यद्रोमाणः; प्रहृष्यन्ति सुखोदयेन भक्त्यतिशयत्वाच्च हर्षयुक्तानि रोमाणि येषाम्; रोमाञ्चितगात्रा इत्यर्थः। पुनः कीदृशाः? **प्रमदसलिलोत्सङ्गितदृशः**; प्रमदसलिलेन प्रमदजलेन प्रमदाश्रुणेति यावत्, उत्सङ्गिता आवृता दृशश्चक्षूंषि येषाम्; आनन्दाश्रुपरिपूर्णनेत्रा इत्यर्थः। विधानं विधिः तेन सह **सविधं** क्रियाविशेषणत्वात् कर्मत्वं सम्यक् विधानयुक्तमित्यर्थः ॥ २५ ॥

इदानीं भगवतः परमतत्त्वनिरूपणमुखेन स्तुवन्नाह—मन इति। हे देव! **यमिनः**; योगिनः, **अन्तः**; आत्मनि, किमपि यत्तत्त्वम्; सच्चिदानन्दरूपम् आलोक्य; **ह्लादम्** सुखम्, दधति; धारयन्ति। किं कृत्वेव? **अमृतमये**; अमृतस्वरूपे, **ह्रदे**; जलाशये, निमज्येव; तत् तत्त्वं भवान् किल त्वमेव, हि। किलशब्दः प्रसिद्धौ। किं कृत्वा? **प्रत्यक्चित्ते**; प्रत्यग्विषयेभ्यो निवृत्ते, अन्तः आत्मनि, मनः, अन्तःकरणम्, **सविधम्**; सप्रकारं, योगशास्त्रोक्तं यथा भवति तथा। **अवधाय**; अवस्थाप्य। किं भूता यमिनः? **आत्तमरुतः**; आत्ताः मरुतः प्राणादिवायवो यैस्तथोक्ताः। पुनः किं भूताः? **प्रहृष्यद्रोमाणः**; प्रहृष्यन्ति रोमाणि पुलकितानि तनूरुहाणि येषां ते तथोक्ताः। पुनः किं भूताः? **प्रमदसलिलोत्सङ्गितदृशः**; प्रमदसलिलैः आनन्दबाष्पैः, उत्सङ्गिताः योजिताः दृशो नेत्राणि येषां ते तथोक्ताः ॥ २६ ॥

इदानीं भगवतोऽष्टमूर्तित्वेन सर्वावयवत्वेन च सर्वात्मकत्वं उद्भावयन् स्तौति—

त्वमर्कस्त्वं सोमस्त्वमसि पवनस्त्वं हुतवह-
स्त्वमापस्त्वं व्योम त्वमु धरणिरात्मा त्वमिति च।
परिच्छिन्नामेवं त्वयि परिणता बिभ्रति गिरं
न विद्मस्तत्तत्त्वं वयमिह हि यत्त्वं न भवसि ॥ २६ ॥

त्वमिति। त्वयि, परमेश्वरेः **परिणताः**; त्वद्भावबुद्धित्वेन परमार्थज्ञतया आत्मानं मन्यमानाः पण्डितजनाः त्वमर्कस्त्वं सोम इत्यादिना परिच्छिन्नां परिमितां गिरं वाणीं बिभ्रति धारयन्ति संस्थापयन्तीति यावत्। वयं तु स्थूलदर्शिनोऽनिपुणा इह संसारे त्वं यद्वस्तु न भवसि तत् अस्तीति न विद्मः न जानीम इति तत्त्वं निश्चितमेवेति। अर्काद्यष्टमूर्त्यात्मकतया वदतां मते, अर्काद्यष्टवस्तु त्वमिति परिमितत्वम्। अस्मन्मते पुनः सर्वमयत्वमिति अपरिमितमिति भेदः। अष्टमूर्तिमाह; **त्वम् अर्कः**;

सूर्यः, ईशानमूर्तिकत्वात् । त्वम् सोमः ; चन्द्रः, महादेवमूर्तिकत्वात् । त्वम् पवनः ; वायुरसि उग्रमूर्तिकत्वात् । त्वम् हुतवहः ; अग्निः, रुद्रमूर्तिकत्वात् । त्वम् आपः ; पयांसि, भवमूर्तिकत्वात् । त्वम् व्योम ; आकाशः ; भीममूर्तिकत्वात् । उ प्रश्ने अप्यर्थे वा । त्वम् धरणिः ; पृथिवी सर्वमूर्तिकत्वात् । त्वम् आत्मा ; यजमानश्च ; पशुपतिमूर्तित्वेनेति । "आत्मैव यजमानः स्याद्विषयापत्तिसंकतौ" इति योगवासिष्ठीयवाक्यात् आत्मा यजमान उच्यते । केचित् आत्मा क्षेत्रज्ञ इति वदन्ति ; तन्न चारु ॥ २६ ॥

सांप्रतमष्टमूर्तिद्वारेण भगवन्तं स्तुवन्नाह—त्वमर्क इति । हे देव ! त्वम् अर्कः ; सूर्योऽसि । त्वम् सोमः ; चन्द्रोऽसि । त्वम् पवनः ; वायुरसि । त्वम् हुतवहः ; अग्निरसि । त्वम् आपः ; उदकमसि । त्वम् व्योम ; आकाशोऽसि । त्वम् धरणिः ; भूमिरसि । उ इति वितर्के । त्वम् आत्मा ; सर्वसाक्षी परमात्मासि । इति च इतिशब्दः समाप्तौ । एवम् ; अनेन प्रकारेण, परिच्छिन्नाम् ; इयत्ताविशिष्टाम्, गिरम् ; वाणीम्, त्वयि विषये, परिणताः ; परिपक्वमतयः, त्वत्स्वरूपविदः ; बिभ्रति ; दधति । वयं तु इह ; लोके, यत् तत्त्वम् ; वस्तु, न त्वम् भवसि, तत् ; तद्वस्तु न जानीमः । "अणोरणीयान् महतो महीयान्" "सर्वं खल्विदं ब्रह्म" इति च श्रुतेः । सद्वा सद्वा भवद्व्यतिरिक्त वस्तु किंचिदपि नास्तीति वयं जानीम एवेत्यर्थः ॥ २६ ॥

इदानीमोंकारस्य समस्तव्यस्ततया प्रतिपाद्यं प्रतिपादयन् स्तौति—

त्रयीं तिस्रो वृत्तीस्त्रिभुवनमथो त्रीनपि सुरा-
नकाराद्यैर्वर्णैस्त्रिभिरभिदधत्तीर्णविकृति ।
तुरीयं ते धाम ध्वनिभिरवरुन्धानमणुभिः
समस्तं व्यस्तं त्वां शरणद गृणात्योमिति पदम् ॥ २७ ॥

त्रयीमिति । हे शरणद ! हे शिव ! ओमिति पदम् ; ओंकारस्वरूपं यदा समस्तम् अकाराद्यैः ; अकारोकारमकारैः त्रिभिर्वर्णैःमिलितं तदा अणुभिः, सूक्ष्मैः, ध्वनिभिः, नादैः, अवरुन्धानम् ; आवृतं नादयुक्तं सत्, त्वां गृणाति आराधयति । तत् पुनरोमिति पदं यदा एवं तदा ते तव तुरीयं धाम चतुर्थं तेजः ब्रह्मस्वरूपस्य तव ब्रह्मविष्णुशिवभेदेन यत् त्रिप्रकारं तेजः ततोऽधिकम्,

तेजो हि चतुर्थं तत् पुनरनिर्वचनीयं नित्यानन्दस्वरूपम् अभिदधत् प्रतिपादयत् अतस्त्वामेव गृणाति तव परमब्रह्मणश्चाभेदात्। धाम कीदृशम्? तीर्णविकृति; तीर्णा उत्क्षिप्ता विकृतयो विकारा येन निर्विकारमित्यर्थः। तथात्र श्रुतिः; "अथासावकारोकारमकारात्मको मिलितः प्रणवत्वेनाविर्भूतो ब्रह्मतेजो वृणीते" इति। यदा पुनरोमिति पदं व्यस्तम्, अकारोकारमकारत्वेन पृथग्भूतं, तदा अकाराद्यैः अकारोकारमकारैस्त्रिभिर्वर्णैरक्षरैः त्रीन् प्रत्येकेनाभिदधत् त्वामेव गृणाति। ब्रह्मणस्तव त्रय्यादिभेदेनाभिन्नत्वात् त्रय्याद्यभिधानेनैव ब्रह्माभिधानात्। त्रयीम् ऋग्यजुः-सामानि वेदान् अभिदधदित्यन्वयः। तथा च गायत्रीकल्पटीकाधृतव्यासवचनम्;

"अकारेणोच्यते ऋक्त्वमुकारेणोच्यते यजुः।
मकारेणोच्यते साम समस्तेनोच्यते परम्॥ इति,

तथा तिस्रो वृत्तीः; सत्त्वरजस्तमोरूपा अभिदधत्। तथाच तत्रैव;

"अकारः सत्त्वमापन्न उकारो रजसांपतिः।
मकारस्तमसां नाथ इति ब्रह्मगुणात्मकम्॥" इति,

"जीवने वर्तने योषिद्वृत्तिर्ब्रह्मगुणेऽपि च" इति शाब्दिकनरसिंहः। तथा त्रिभुवनम् स्वर्गमर्त्यपातालमभिदधत्। तथा च श्रुतिः, 'अथातो वर्णत्रयात् स्वर्गमर्त्यपातालानामभिधा नाम जानीते' इति। तथा त्रीनपि सुरान्; ब्रह्मविष्णुशिवान् अभिदधत्। तथा च वर्णदेशना; 'अकारो ब्रह्म चाख्यात उकारो विष्णुरीरितः' इति शब्दार्णवः। "मकारः कामहारकः" इति मन्त्राभिधानम्। एतेन ओमिति पदं समस्तमपि त्वां गृणाति; किंत्वेतावांस्तु विशेषः; यदा समस्तं तदा अभेदेनैव अभिन्नं तेजोरूपं त्वां गृणाति; व्यस्तं चेत् भेदेन विभिन्नत्वं त्रय्यादिरूपं त्वामेव गृणातीत्यर्थः। यद्यपि विभिन्नवर्णस्वभावेन ओमिति पदम् एकस्वरूपं न संभवति, तदानीं प्रत्येकस्य पदत्वात्; तथापि ओमिति समस्तघटकीभूतप्रत्येकाकारादिवर्णस्य ओमिति पदत्वमुक्तमिति ध्येयम्। केचित्तु ओमिति पदं यदा समस्तं समासनिष्पादितम् अकारश्च उकारश्च मकारश्चेति द्वन्द्वसमासनिष्पादितं तदा त्वां गृणाति। यदा पुनर्व्यस्तं समासनिष्पादितभिन्नं, "अवतेरन्त्यस्वरादिलोपश्च" इत्यनेन साधितं तदापि त्वमेव गृणाति इत्यर्थं कुर्वन्ति॥ २७॥

इदानीं प्रणवप्रतिपाद्यत्वेन भगवन्तं स्तोतुमाह—त्रयीमिति। हे शरणद! **ओमिति पदम्**; प्रणवः। ओमिति पदं किं भूतम्? **समस्तम्**; समस्तरूपेणाखण्डरूपेण व्यापकम्। **व्यस्तम्**; व्यस्तरूपेण खण्डरूपेणाक्षयविभागेन व्याप्यम्। **त्वाम् गृणाति**; स्तौति। पुनः किं विधम्? अकाराद्यैः वर्णैः त्रिभिः; अकारोकारमकारैः, एतान्, **अभिदधत्**; एतानि कानि? त्रयीम्; ऋग्यजुःसामानि, तिस्रः वृत्तीः; त्रीन् स्वरान्, उदात्तानुदात्तस्वरितान्; त्रिभुवनम्ः त्रैलोक्यम्; अथो; अनन्तरम्, त्रीन सुरानपि; ब्रह्मविष्णुरुद्रान्; अकारेण ऋगुदात्तस्वर्गब्रह्माण अभिधीयन्ते। तथा उकारेण सामानुदात्तमर्त्यविष्णव अभिधीयन्ते। तथा मकारेण यजुर्वेदस्वरितपातालरुद्रा अभिधीयन्ते। पुनः किंविधमोंकारम्? ते; तव, तुरीयं धाम; स्थानं तेजो वा; अणुभिरिति, सूक्ष्मैः ध्वनिभिः अवरुन्धानं व्याप्नुवत्। किंभूतं तुरीयं धाम? तीर्णविकृति; तीर्णा विकृतिर्येन तत्, तीणविकृति; विकाररहितमित्यर्थः ॥ २७ ॥

इदानीं भगवतः प्रधाननामाष्टकमुद्भावयन् स्तौति—

भवः शर्वो रुद्रः पशुपतिरथोग्रः सह महां-
स्तथा भीमेशानाविति यदभिधानाष्टकमिदम्।
अमुष्मिन् प्रत्येकं प्रविचरति देवः श्रुतिरपि
प्रियायास्मै नाम्ने प्रणिहितनमस्योऽस्मि भवते ॥ २८ ॥

भव इति। हे शिव! भव इत्यादि यदिदं अभिधानाष्टकम् **अमुष्मिन्** नामाष्टके देवो महादेवः **प्रविचरति** प्रत्येकमधितिष्ठति भ्रमतीति यावत्। तथा **श्रुतिरपि** वेदोऽपि **प्रत्येकं** प्रविचरति। अतः **अस्मै नाम्ने** अहं **प्रणिहितनमस्यः** संपादितनमस्कारोऽस्मि भवामि। नाम्ने कीदृशाय? **प्रियाय** नामसहस्रेषु प्राधान्यात् तव प्रियकराय। पुनः कीदृशाय? **भवते** प्रकाशं कुर्वते भातेर्डवतुः, ततश्चतुर्थी। यद्वा—अमुष्मिन् नामाष्टके देवः शिवः प्रविचरति, श्रुतिरपि अस्मै नाम्ने नामतदर्थाय प्रविचरति प्रकर्षेण विचरति धावति। एतन्नामाष्टकं संचेतुं सत्वरो भवतीति भावः। अत्र पक्षे—हे भव! ते तुभ्यं कृतनमस्कारो भवामीत्यर्थः। नामाष्टकमाह—भव इत्यादि। **सह महान्** महादेवेन सह उग्र इत्यन्वयः। महान् इत्यनेन महादेव उच्यते, यथा भीमो भीमसेनः। तथा च विष्णुपुराणे,

"रुद्रस्त्वं देव नामासि मा रोदीर्धैर्यमावह ।
भवं शर्वमथेशानं तथा पशुपतिं द्विज ।
भीममुग्रं महादेवमुवाच स पितामहः ॥" इति ॥

"आख्याह्वे चाभिधानं च नामधेयं च नाम च" इत्यमरः । "वेदे श्रवसि च श्रुतिः" इत्यमरः ॥ २८ ॥

इदानीं नामाष्टकप्रतिपादनद्वारेण भगवन्तं स्तुवन्नाह—भव इति । हे देव! यदिदं तव भवाद्यभिधानाष्टकम् अमुष्मिन् नामाष्टके प्रत्येकम्; एकमेकं प्रति, श्रुतिरपि वेदोऽपि, प्रविचरति प्रवर्तते । तत्किमभिधानाष्टकम्? तदेवाह—भवः; शर्वः; रुद्रः; पशुपतिः; अथ; अनन्तरम्, उग्रः; स च महानित्युक्त्या महादेव उच्यते । तथा भीमेशानौ इति हेतोः प्रियायास्मै धाम्ने पूर्वश्लोकप्रतिपादिताय तेजोरूपाय, भवते; तुभ्यम्, प्रणिहितनमस्योऽस्मि; कृतनमस्कारोऽस्मि । अथवा, हे भव! तव प्रियायास्मै धाम्ने तुरीयतेजसे प्रणिहितनमस्योऽस्मि, कृतनमस्कारोऽस्मि ॥ २८ ॥

इदानीं परस्परविरुद्धधर्मत्वमुद्भावयन् स्तौति—

नमो नेदिष्ठाय प्रियदव दविष्ठाय च नमो
नमः क्षोदिष्ठाय स्मरहर महिष्ठाय च नमः ।
नमो वंहिष्ठाय त्रिनयन यविष्ठाय च नमो
नमः सर्वस्मै ते तदिदमतिसर्वाय च नमः ॥ २९ ॥

नम इत्यादि । हे प्रियदव! हे प्रियदावाग्ने, नेदिष्ठाय सर्वभूतगामित्वात् अतिनिकटवर्त्तिने ते तुभ्यं नमः । तथा दविष्ठाय वाङ्मनसोरतीतविषयत्वेन दुरधिगम्यत्वात् अतिदूरस्थाय तुभ्यं नमः । "नेदिष्ठमन्तिकतमम्", "दवदावौ वनारण्यवह्नी", "दवीयश्च दविष्ठं च" इत्यमरः । नेदिष्ठेति, "अन्तिकबाढयोर्नेदसाधौ" इत्यन्तिकस्य नेदादेशः । दविष्ठेति, "स्थूलदूरयुवह्रस्वक्षिप्रक्षुद्राणाम्" इत्यादिना अन्तस्थादेर्लोपो गुणश्चेति । अत्र दूरस्थनिकटस्थत्वेन विरुद्धधर्मित्वम् । तथा हे स्मरहर! क्षोदिष्ठाय परमाण्वादिरूपेणातिक्षुद्राय तुभ्यं नमः । तथा महिष्ठाय पर्वतादिरूपेणातिमहद्रूपाय अतिपरिमाणदेहायेति यावत् । ते तुभ्यं नमः । अत्रातिसूक्ष्मातिस्थूलयोर्विरुद्धत्वम् । क्षोदिष्ठेति क्षुद्रशब्दस्य पूर्ववदन्तस्थादेर्लोपो

गुणश्च। महिष्ठेति महच्छब्दस्य तद्धत्, "तुरिष्ठेमेयःसु" इति कारितवद्भावादन्त्य-स्वरादिलोपः। तथा हे **त्रिनयन!** **बंहिष्ठाय** सर्वेषामादिभूतत्वात् वृद्धतमाय नमः। तथा **यविष्ठाय** जरापरिणामादिदोषैरस्पृष्टत्वात् सर्वकार्यक्षमत्वाच्च अतियुवकाय तुभ्यं नमः। अत्रापि वृद्धत्वयौवनत्वयोर्विरुद्धत्वम्। बंहिष्ठेति "प्रियस्थिर"—इत्यादिना वृद्धस्य बंहादेश इति धातुपारायणः। तन्मते गणसूत्रे बंहादेशस्योक्तत्वात्। अस्मन्मते वर्षादेशस्य स्वीकारात् वर्षिष्ठाय इत्यपरः पाठः। यविष्ठेति युवन्शब्दस्य पूर्ववदन्त-स्यादेर्लोपो गुणश्च। तथा सर्वस्मै परोक्षापरोक्षसर्वपदार्थत्वात् साकल्यरूपाय तुभ्यं नमः। तथा **अतिसर्वाय;** वाङ्मनसोरतीतविषयत्वात् सर्वमतिक्रान्ताय च तुभ्यं नमः। अत्रापि सर्वातिक्रान्तत्वसर्वत्वयोर्विरुद्धत्वम् अतिसर्वायेत्युपसर्जनत्वान्न सर्वनामत्वम् ॥ २९ ॥

इदानीं भगवतः प्रकटरूपतां प्रतिपादयन्नाह—नमो नेदिष्ठायेति। नेदिष्ठाय; अन्तिकतमाय, शिवाय नमः; निकटवर्तिने तुभ्यं नम इत्यर्थः। हे प्रियदव! प्रियो दवो यस्य सः; प्रियदवः, तस्य संबुद्धिः। दविष्ठाय; दूरतमाय, शिवाय नमः, अतिदूरस्था-येति यावत्। तथा क्षोदिष्ठाय; सूक्ष्मतराय नमः। हे स्मरहर! महिष्ठाय; महत्तमाय च नमः। तथा वर्षिष्ठाय; वृद्धतराय ते नमः। हे त्रिनयन! यविष्ठाय; युवतराय ते तुभ्यं नमः। तथा सर्वस्मै ते नमः। तथा अतिसर्वाय; सर्वमतिक्रान्ताय, तदिदम्; नमः; अयं नमस्कार इत्यर्थः ॥ २९ ॥

इदानीं त्रिगुणात्मकतया सृष्टिस्थितिप्रलयकर्तृत्वं गुणातीतत्वेन परमब्रह्मत्वं च उद्भावयन् स्तौति—

बहुलरजसे विश्वोत्पत्तौ भवाय नमो नमः
प्रबलतमसे तत्संहारे हराय नमो नमः।
जनसुखकृते सत्त्वस्थित्यै मृडाय नमो नमः
प्रमहसि पदे निस्त्रैगुण्ये शिवाय नमो नमः ॥ ३० ॥

बहुल इत्यादि। भवत्यस्मादिति भवो ब्रह्मा भवाय सृष्टिकर्त्रे तुभ्यं नमः। कीदृशाय? **विश्वोत्पत्तौ** जगदुत्पत्तिविषये बहुलं यथेष्टं रजो गुणो यस्य तस्मै रजो-गुणात्मने इत्यर्थः। तथा हरति विश्वमिति हरो रुद्रः, तस्मै **हराय नमो नमः।** तत्

तस्य विश्वस्य संहारे प्रलयविषये प्रबलमनिर्वचनीयं तमो गुणो यस्य तस्मै तमोगुणात्मने इत्यर्थः। तथा मृडयति सुखयतीति मृडः विश्वपालकत्वात् विष्णुरूपः, तस्मै नमो नमः। कीदृशाय? सत्त्वस्थित्यै आत्मनि सत्त्वगुणस्थितिः, तदर्थाय। जनानां सुखं करोतीति क्विप्; तस्मै सत्त्वगुणाधारतया विश्वपालकत्वेनैव जनसुखकर्त्रे इत्यर्थः। यद्वा—सत्त्वेन सत्वगुणेन स्थितिं पालनं कर्तुं जनसुखं कर्म, "नित्यं कर्मणि तुमोऽप्रयोगिन" इति चतुर्थी। तथा प्रमहसि प्रकृष्टतेजोरूपे पदे वस्तुनि अर्थादधिष्ठाने परमब्रह्मणे शिवाय नमो नमः। पदे कीदृशे? त्रिगुणा एव त्रैगुण्यं स्वार्थे यण्; निर्गतं त्रैगुण्यात् निस्त्रैगुण्यं तस्मिन् अतीतगुणत्रये इत्यर्थः। "महस्तूत्सवतेजसोः" इत्यमरः। "पदं व्यवसितत्राणस्थानलक्ष्माङ्घ्रिवस्तुषुः" इत्यमरः। भक्त्युद्रेकेण विस्मयेन हर्षेण च नमः। पदबाहुल्यमित्यपौनरुक्तम्। तथा च "विवादे विस्मये हर्षे द्विस्त्रिरुक्तिर्न दुष्यति" इति दृश्यते। "सत्त्वं गुणे पिशाचादौ" इत्यमरः;॥३०॥

इदानीं सांख्यपातञ्जलप्रक्रियां स्तुवन्नाह—बहुलरजस इति। रजोगुणः उत्पत्तिहेतुः, तमोगुणः नाशहेतुः, सत्त्वगुणः रक्षणहेतुः। ईश्वरः यदा उत्पत्तिं करोति, तदा रजोगुणयुक्तो भवति। यदा नाशाय प्रभवति, तदा तमोगुणयुक्तो भवति। यदा हितं करोति, तदा सत्त्वगुणयुक्तो भवति। एतदाश्रित्याह—विश्वेति। विश्वोत्पत्तौ; जगत्सृष्टौ कर्तव्यायां सत्याम्, बहुलरजसे; अधिकरजोगुणाय भवाय नमो नमः। जगदुत्पत्तेः भवरूपत्वात् तदनुगुणेन भवशब्देन नमस्कारः कृतः। सत्त्वोद्रेके; जगत्पालनसुखकारणसत्त्वगुणोद्रेके, जनसुखकृते; लोकहितकराय सत्वगुणयुक्ताय मृडाय नमो नमः। सत्त्वगुणस्य सुखहेतुत्वात् तदनुगुणेन मृडशब्देन नमस्कारः कृतः। सत्त्वस्थित्यै इत्यपि पाठः। तत्संहारे; जगन्नाशे, प्रबलतमसे; अधिकतमोगुणयुक्ताय, हराय नमो नमः। तमोगुणस्य नाशहेतुत्वात् हरति संहरति जगदिति व्युत्पत्त्या हरशब्दो निष्पन्नः। अतः तदनुगुणेन हरशब्देन नमस्कारः कृतः। तथा प्रमहसि; प्रकृष्टतेजसि, निस्त्रैगुण्ये; गुणत्रयातीते, पदे; स्थाने, शिवाय नमो नमः। यदा सृष्ट्यादिर्नास्ति, तदा सत्त्वादिगुणाभावात् परस्य शिवस्य निस्त्रैगुण्यं भवति। अतः तस्य तदा केवलमङ्गलरूपत्वात् तदुचितेन शिवशब्देन नमस्कारः कृतः। नमो नम इति भक्त्यतिशयेन वीप्सायां द्विर्भावः॥ ३० ॥

इदानीमात्मनो विनयमुद्भावयन् स्तौति—

कृशपरिणति चेतः क्लेशवश्यं क्व चेदं

क्व च तव गुणसीमोल्लङ्घिनी शश्वदृद्धिः।

इति चकितममन्दीकृत्य मां भक्तिराधा-
द्वरद चरणयोस्ते वाक्यपुष्पोपहारम् ॥ ३१ ॥

कृशेति । हे वरद! **कृशपरिणति;** कृशा क्षीणा परिणतिः परिणामो गम्यो यस्य, अल्पगम्यमिति यावत् । तादृशं मम **इदं चेतः** मनः क? । चेतः कीदृशम्? **क्लेशवश्यम्;** क्लेशस्य दुःखस्य अधीनं दुःखेन जडीभूतम्, **शश्वत्** वारं वारं **गुणसीमोल्लङ्घिनी;** गुणसीमानं गुणानामियत्तापरिच्छेदं उल्लङ्घयितुम् अतिक्रमयितुं शीलं यस्याः तादृशी **तव ऋद्धिः** समृद्धिर्वा क? । एतादृशी तव समृद्धिः ममाल्पविषयचेतसोऽगम्येति अत्यन्तासंभावनायां द्वौ कौ प्रयुक्तौ । अत्रापि **इति** हेतोः **चकितं** भीतं **मां भक्तिः** कर्त्री, **अमन्दीकृत्य** निःशङ्कीकृत्य, **ते** तव **चरणयोः** पादयुगले **आधात्** अर्पितवती । यद्यपि तव चरणारविन्दस्तुतिकरणे मम चेतसोऽयोग्यतेति हेतोरहं भीतोऽस्मि; तथापि त्वच्चरणयोः मम या भक्तिः सैव मां निर्भीकं कृत्वा बलात्कारेणैव अर्पितवतीति भक्तिर्बलवतीति ध्वनितम् । मां कीदृशम्? **वाक्यपुष्पोपहारम्;** वाक्यमेव पुष्पोपहारः कुसुमबलिर्यस्य, वाक्यं स्तुतिः सैव पादपूजायां पुष्पोपहार इत्यर्थः । अमन्दीकृत्येति च्विप्रत्ययः ॥ ३१ ॥

इदानीमभिप्रेतार्थसिद्धौ सत्यामात्मीयमौद्धत्यं परिहरन्नाह—**कृशेति** । **इदम्;** मदीयम्, **चेतः;** मानसं क? किंभूतं मानसम्? **कृशपरिणति;** कृशा परिणतिः परिणामो यस्य तत्; स्वल्पविचारगोचरमित्यर्थः । तथा **क्लेशवश्यम्;** दुःखपराधीनम् । **तव ऋद्धिः** महिमा क? किं भूता ऋद्धिः? **शश्वत्;** सर्वदा, **गुणसीमोल्लङ्घिनी;** गुणमर्यादातिक्रान्ता । **इति;** अनेन प्रकारेण, **चकितम्;** भीतम् **माम्,** हे **वरद! ते;** तव, **चरणयोः भक्तिः अमन्दीकृत्य;** भीतिरहितं कृत्वा, **वाक्यपुष्पोपहारम्;** वाक्यानि पुष्पाणीव तेषामुपहारं पूजाम्; यद्वा—वाक्यान्येव पुष्पाणि, तेषामुपहारं पूजाम् **आधात्** अकल्पयत् ॥ ३१ ॥

इदानीमृद्धेर्गुणसीमोल्लङ्घनीयत्वमासादयति—

असितगिरिसमं स्यात्कज्जलं सिन्धुपात्रे
सुरतरुवरशाखा लेखनी पत्रमुर्वी ।
लिखति यदि गृहीत्वा शारदा सर्वकालं
तदपि तव गुणानामीश पारं न याति ॥ ३२ ॥

असितेति। हे ईश! **असितगिरिसमम्**; यदि असितगिरेर्नीलपर्वतस्य समं तुल्यं **कज्जलं** मषी स्यात्। कज्जलं कीदृशम्? **सिन्धुपात्रम्**; सिन्धुः समुद्रः पात्रं मष्याधारो यस्य तादृशम्। **सुरतरुवरशाखा**; तथा सुरतरोः पारिजातवृक्षस्य वरशाखा प्रधानशाखा यदि **लेखनी** स्यात्; तथा **उर्वी** पृथ्वी यदि **पत्रं** स्यात्; एतानतिबृहत्तया चिरस्थायिनो **गृहीत्वा** आदाय **शारदा** सरस्वती **सर्वकालं** युगमन्वादिरूपं व्याप्य **लिखति, गुणानां** लेखनं करोति, **तदपि** तथापि तव **गुणानां पारं** पर्यन्तं **न याति** न प्राप्नोति। एतेन तादृशसामग्रीसहकारेण सरस्वत्यपि तव गुणानां इयत्तापरिच्छेदं कर्तुं न शक्नोति; कथमल्पविषयचेतसामस्माकं तत्रारम्भ इति गुणकीर्तनविषये सर्व एव कुण्ठाः; तथापि तत्र यदारम्भः तत्र भक्तेरेव वलवत्ता कारणमिति पूर्वश्लोकेन ध्वनितम्। "वाग्वाणी शारदा सत्या ब्रह्मपत्नी सरस्वती" इति व्याडिः॥ ३२॥

असितेति। हे **ईश! असितगिरिसमम्**; नीलगिरितुल्यम्, **कज्जलम्**; अञ्जनम्, स्याद्यदि; क्व? सिन्धुपात्रे, यदि सुरतरुवरशाखा लेखिनी स्यात्, यदि उर्वी भूमिः; पत्रं स्याद्यदि; यदि शारदा सरस्वती स्वयमुर्वीपत्रं गृहीत्वा सार्वकालं लिखति। तदपि तव गुणानां पारम् अन्तं न याति न प्राप्नोति॥ ३२॥

इदानीं स्तवप्रकाशे कारणमासादयति—

कुसुमदशननामा सर्वगन्धर्वराजः
शिशुशशधरमौलेर्देवदेवस्य दासः।
स खलु निजमहिम्नो भ्रष्ट एवास्य रोषात्
स्तवनमिदमकार्षीद्दिव्यदिव्यं महिम्नः॥ ३३॥

कुसुमेति। **कुसुमदशननामा**; कुसुमानीव दशना दन्ता यस्य स कुसुमदशनः पुष्पदन्तः स एव नाम यस्य स पुष्पदन्तनामा; **सर्वगन्धर्वाणां राजा, देवदेवस्य** शिवस्य **दासः** अभूत्। **अस्य** शिवस्य **रोषात्** निर्माल्यपादस्पर्शनेन कोपात् **निजमहिम्नः**; गगनचरणादिस्वकीयमहिमतः, **भ्रष्टः**; च्युतः सन्, **इदं महिम्नः स्तवनम्**; **अकार्षीत्** प्रकाशितवान्। देवदेवस्य कीदृशस्य? **शिशुशशधर-**

मौलेः; शिशुर्बालः शशधरश्चन्द्रमौलौ शिरसि यस्य; अर्धचन्द्रखण्डभूषितस्येत्यर्थः। स्तवनं कीदृशम्? दिव्यात् मनोज्ञात् दिव्यं मनोज्ञं अतिमनोज्ञमिति यावत् ॥ ३३ ॥

इदानीं महिम्नस्तवपाठफलमाह—

सुरगुरुमभिपूज्य स्वर्गमोक्षैकहेतुं
पठति यदि मनुष्यः प्राञ्जलिर्नान्यचेताः।
व्रजति शिवसमीपं किंनरैः स्तूयमानः
स्तवनमिदममोघं पुष्पदन्तप्रणीतम् ॥ ३४ ॥

सुरगुरुमिति। सुरगुरुम्; सुराणां देवतानां गुरुं महादेवम्, अभिपूज्य; पूजयित्वा, प्राञ्जलिः; कृताञ्जलिः सन्, यदि पुष्पदन्तप्रणीतम्; पुष्पदन्तेन प्रकाशितम्; इदं स्तवनम्; स्तोत्रं पठति, तदा स जनः किंनरैः स्तूयमानः सन्, शिवसमीपं व्रजति गच्छति। सुरगुरुं कीदृशम्? स्वर्गमोक्षैकहेतुम्; स्वर्गस्य मोक्षस्य च एकहेतुं मुख्यकारणम्; स्वर्गमोक्षकारणीभूतशिवसमीपगमनेनैव स्वर्गमोक्षमपि लभत इति भावः। मनुष्यः कीदृशः सन् पठति? नान्यचेताः; न विद्यते अन्यस्मिन् विषये चेतो मनो यस्य तादृशः अनन्यचित्त इत्यर्थः। (स्वरेऽक्षरविपर्यय इति नाक्षरविपर्ययः वक्ष्यमाणकचिदधिकारस्वीकारात् ?) स्तवनं कीदृशम्? अमोघम्; अव्यर्थं शिवसमीपगमने अव्यर्थकारणमित्यर्थः। "मोघो व्यर्थे खले पुमान्" इति शब्दार्णवः। "एके मुख्यान्यकेवला" इत्यमरः ॥ ३४ ॥

अन्यदपि फलमाह—

श्रीपुष्पदन्तमुखपङ्कजनिर्गतेन
स्तोत्रेण किल्बिषहरेण हरप्रियेण।
कण्ठस्थितेन पठितेन गृहस्थितेन
संप्रीणितो भवति भूतपतिर्महेशः ॥ ३५ ॥

इति श्रीपुष्पदन्तगन्धर्वराजविरचितं हरमहिम्नस्तोत्रं समाप्तम्।

श्रीपुष्पदन्तेति। अनेन **स्तोत्रेण**; स्तवेन, **कण्ठस्थितेन**; कण्ठायत्तेन, **पठितेन**; आवृत्तेन **गृहस्थितेन**; पुस्तकलिखिततया **गृहस्थितेन** च, **भूतपतिः**; भूतानां प्राणिनां पतिः, **महेशः**; शिवः, **संप्रीणितो** भवति। अस्मिन् प्रीणिते सकलपुरुषार्थसिद्धिरिति भावः। कीदृशेन स्तोत्रेण? **श्रीपुष्पदन्तमुखपङ्कजनिर्गतेन**; पुष्पदन्तस्य गन्धर्वराजस्य मुखपङ्कजान्निर्गतेन पूर्वं देवप्रतिपादितमपि गुप्तमासीत्, पश्चादनेन प्रकाशितमिति भावः। एतेनानादित्वमस्येति तात्पर्यम्। पुनः कीदृशेन? **किल्बिषहरेण**; पापनाशकेन। पुनः कीदृशेन? **हरप्रियेण**; हरस्य शिवस्य प्रियेण प्रीतिजनकेन॥ ३५ ॥

इति श्रीजगन्नाथचक्रवर्त्तिविरचिता हरमहिम्नस्तोत्रटीका समाप्ता।

इदानीं स्वजन्मकृतमपराधक्षमापनं याचते—

वपुःप्रादुर्भावादनुमितमिदं जन्मनि पुरा
पुरारे न क्वापि क्षणमपि भवन्तं प्रणतवान्।
नमन्मुक्तः सम्प्रत्यहमतनुरग्रेऽप्यनतिमा-
नितीश क्षन्तव्यं तदिदमपराधद्वयमपि॥ ३३ ॥[1]

वपुरिति। हे पुरारे! **वपुःप्रादुर्भावात्**; वपुषः प्रादुर्भावात्, **इदम्**; वक्ष्यमाणम्; **अनुमितम्**; ऊहितम्। किं तत्? **क्वापि जन्मनि**; कस्मिंश्चित् जन्मन्यपीत्यर्थः। **पुरा**; पूर्वम्, **क्षणमपि**; त्रुटिकालमपि, अत्यन्तसंयोगे द्वितीया। **भवन्तं न प्रणतवान्।** पूर्वजन्मनि तव प्रणामो यदि क्रियते, तर्हि इदानीं शरीरप्रादुर्भावो न स्यात्। इदानीं शरीरप्रादुर्भावात् पूर्वजन्मनि भवतः प्रणामो न कृत इति निश्चितम्। संप्रति भवन्तं प्रति, **नमन्** नमस्कुर्वन्, **अतनुः** अधिकः सन्; यद्वा—अतनुः अशरीरः सन् **मुक्तः** मुक्तिं गतः। अत एव **अग्रेऽपि अनतिमान्** नमस्कारम् अकृतवान् अभवम्। इदानीं तव नमस्कारात् मुक्तत्वेन अग्रेऽपि देहादेरभावात् अनतिमान् इति मया कृतम् अपराधद्वयम्; इदानीं शरीरप्रादुर्भावात् पूर्वजन्मनि तव नमस्कारो मया न कृत इत्येकोऽपराधः; इदानीं नमस्कुर्वन् मुक्तत्वेन मम पुनर्देहादेरभावात् तवाग्रेऽपि नमस्कारो न कृत इत्येकोऽपराधः; तदिदम् अपराधद्वयम् इदानीं हे ईश क्षन्तव्यम्॥ ३२ ॥

[1] अत्र सारदीपिकानुसारेणेमे श्लोकाः संगृहीताः

इदानीं स्वकृतस्तोत्रस्य महिमानं प्रस्तौति—

असुरसुरमुनीन्द्रैरर्चितस्येन्दुमौलेः
प्रथितगुणमहिम्नो निर्गुणस्येश्वरस्य ।
सकलगुणवरिष्ठः पुष्पदन्ताभिधानो
रुचिरमलघुवृत्तैः स्तोत्रमेतच्चकार ॥ ३४ ॥

असुरेति । सकलगुणवरिष्ठः ; सर्वामरश्रेष्ठः, पुष्पदन्ताभिधानः ; असुरसुरमुनीन्द्रैः ; अर्चितस्य पूजितस्य, इन्दुमौलेः ; चन्द्रमौलेः, प्रथितगुणमहिम्नः ; प्रथिताः प्रसिद्धाः गुणाः सत्त्वादयो यस्य, महिमा ऐश्वर्यं यस्य, तस्य सगुणात्मकत्वेन प्रसिद्धस्येत्यर्थः । निर्गुणस्य ; वस्तुतो गुणरहितस्य, ईश्वरस्य ; परमेश्वरस्य, अलघुवृत्तैः ; अलघुभिः गुरुभिः ; वृत्तैः चरित्रैः, यद्वा—अलघुवृत्तैः, छन्दोमयवृत्तैः, शिखरिणीवृत्तैरित्यर्थः । रुचिरम् ; शोभनम्, एतत् स्तोत्रं चकार ॥ ३३ ॥

संप्रति स्तवपठनस्य फलमाह—

अहरहरनवद्यं धूर्जटेः स्तोत्रमेत-
त्पठति परमभक्त्या शुद्धचित्तः पुमान्यः ।
स भवति शिवलोके रुद्रतुल्यस्तथेह
प्रचुरतरधनायुः पुत्रवान्कीर्तिमांश्च ॥ ३५ ॥

अहरहरिति । यः पुमान् धूर्जटेः ईश्वरस्य अनवद्यम् सकलगुणसमृद्धम् एतत् स्तोत्रम् परमभक्त्या शुद्धचित्तः सन् अहरहः पठति, सः, पुमान्, इह अस्मिन् भूलोके, प्रचुरतरधनायुः ; प्रचुरतरं धनम् आयुर्यस्य, तथाभूतः सन्, पुत्रवान्, कीर्तिमांश्च सन्, तथा रुद्रतुल्यः ; रुद्रेण ईश्वरेण तुल्यः शिवलोके वसति ॥ ३४ ॥

अधुना स्तवस्यास्य दीक्षादानादिभ्योऽप्यधिकफलमाह—

दीक्षा दानं तपस्तीर्थं ज्ञानं यागादिकाः क्रियाः ।
महिम्नस्तवपाठस्य कलां नार्हन्ति षोडशीम् ॥ ३६ ॥

दीक्षेति । दीक्षा ; शिवदीक्षा, दानम् ; तुलापुरुषादिदानम्, तप: ; अनशनादि-नियम:, तीर्थम् ; गङ्गादिपुण्यतीर्थसेवनम्, ज्ञानम् ; वेदान्तश्रवणजन्यम्, यज्ञादिका: क्रिया: ; यज्ञादिसत्कर्माणि, महिम्नस्तवपाठस्य ईश्वरस्य महिम्नस्तवजपस्य, षोडशीं कलां नार्हन्ति । दीक्षादिभ्योऽप्यधिकफलप्रदमेतत्स्तोत्रपठनमिति भाव: ॥ ३९ ॥

इदानीं महेशस्य सर्वातिशायिनं महिमानमाविष्कुर्वन् स्तवमुपसंहरति—

महेशान्नापरो देवो महिम्नो नापरास्तुतिः ।
अघोरान्नापरो मन्त्रो नास्ति तत्त्वं गुरोः परम् ॥ ३७ ॥

इति श्रीपुष्पदन्तविरचितं महिम्नस्तोत्रं समाप्तम्

महेशादिति । महेशात् अन्यो देवो नास्ति । महिम्न: अपरा स्तुति: नास्ति । अघोरात् मन्त्रात् अपरो मन्त्रो नास्ति । गुरो: परमन्यत् तत्त्वं वस्तु नास्ति । यथा शिव: सर्वोत्तम:, तथेयं स्तुतिरपीति भाव: ॥ ३६ ॥

एवमेषा कृता व्याख्या मया सारार्थदीपिका ।
अर्पिता चरणाम्भोजे शंकरस्य शुभावहा ॥

सारार्थदीपिका समाप्ता ।

अन्यैर्व्याख्यातृभिः संगृहीताः श्लोकाः—

असमाप्तमिदं स्तोत्रं पुण्यं गन्धर्वभाषितम् ।
अनौपम्यं मनोहारि शिवमीश्वरवर्णनम् ॥

इत्येषा वाङ्मयी पूजा श्रीमच्छंकरपादयोः ।
अर्पिता तेन देवेशः प्रीयतां मे सदाशिवः ॥

तव तत्त्वं न जानामि कीदृशोऽसि महेश्वरम् ।
यादृशोऽसि महादेव तादृशाय नमो नमः ॥

एककालं द्विकालं वा त्रिकालं यः पठेन्नरः ।
सर्वपापविनिर्मुक्तः शिवलोके महीयते ॥

महिम्नस्तोत्रपद्यानामनुक्रमः

व्याख्यानोदाहृतप्रमाणवाक्यानामनुक्रम:

महिम्नस्तोत्रम्